Turkeyneck Hill
and Beyond

PHYLLIS DOW BEX

Foreword by Joyce Long

Name: Phyllis Dow Bex
Title: Turkeyneck Hill and Beyond
Identifiers:
ISBN: 9798989685295 (paperback)
        9798991359016 (hard cover)
        9798991359023 (e-book)
Library of Congress Control Number: 2025902908

Book cover design: Francine Eden Platt • Eden Graphics, Inc.

Book cover photo: Supan Family Farm in Toluca, Illinois. Farmed by Anthony and Mary Supan (husband and wife), and Dave Supan (Anthony's brother)

All Scripture quotations, unless otherwise indicated, are taken from the Holy Bible, New International Version®, NIV®. Copyright ©1973, 1978, 1984, 2011 by Biblica, Inc.™ Used by permission of Zondervan. All rights reserved worldwide. www.zondervan.com The "NIV" and "New International Version" are trademarks registered in the United States Patent and Trademark Office by Biblica, Inc.™

Published by
Never Alone Publishing
Fort Wayne, IN

Be strong and courageous. Do not be afraid; Do not be discouraged, for the Lord your God will be with you wherever you go.

Joshua 1:9 NIV

Dedications

To my respected loved ones:

Katte and David

Maisy Rose

Kitte and Mike

Jessica Ann

George and Lily

Lois and Dick

Carol and Jim

Philip and Patty

Georgiann

In tender memory of:

Mom and Dad

Aunt Bessie

Our precious sister, Clara

Foreword

Not often does a complete stranger approach, introduce herself, and then look you straight in the eye with this declaration: "I want to be you."

A bit taken back, I remember cocking my head and spitting out a profound, "What?"

To our mutual credit, it didn't take long to figure out that Phyllis Bex wanted help in learning to write and publish. And if you know Phyllis at all, you know that once she sets a goal, she pursues it full throttle. For me and the rest of our encouraging critique group, the Heartland Christian Writers, we were blessed to be a part of her journey eight years ago. As they say, the rest is history.

Relatable and laughable stories make book three of her Life on Turkeyneck Hill trilogy fun. My favorites are found in the first two sections because I love animals and can relate to their calamities as country dwellers. Plus, why not laugh rather than cry at the challenges of aging? Dying on the Toilet could win a countrywoman's Pulitzer Prize.

But as required with any significant success, Phyllis has rolled up her sleeves and put a multitude of hours into researching, writing, editing, and marketing. The Taylor University Professional Writing Conference in July 2023 provided the added blessing of Never Alone Publishing directed by Kim Autrey. Hundreds of newspaper columns and three books later, Phyllis has achieved her publishing goal.

While it's been my blessing and pleasure to watch her evolve as a writer, the bigger blessing has blossomed into a forever friendship anchored in our Lord and Savior, Jesus Christ. Phyllis, He's anointed your pen/keyboard so keep writing, my dear friend!

Joyce Long
Heartland Christian Writers, Greenwood, IN
Real Mothers: A bible study about Mothers for Mothers
(2009 - CrossLink Publishing)
Trinity: Walk in Love, Forgiveness and Peace
(2018 – CrossLink Publishing)

A Note from the Author

Welcome to the third book about Turkeyneck Hill. Only this time it contains several stories unrelated to the farm and country life. Still, I attempt to make the narratives practical with a real lift to the everyday life. So, I call it "Beyond."

Thank you—if you have read my first two books, *Life on Turkeyneck Hill: A Memoir* and the second, *More Tales from Turkeyneck Hill*. My sincere thanks for your purchase, read, and review. And if you haven't, it isn't too late.

My steadfast hope is the third book will continue to inspire, inform, cause laughter and tears, but most importantly— that these stories cause you to remember your own stories of life. Anytime a word can enable you to draw closer to friends and family, heal the gaps, and bridge the memories, it is a good word.

Of course, many of these stories have been published in the newspaper but some have never been printed. Perhaps you will be aptly surprised by some. Feel free to share my stories if they bring joy to you and then results in joy for another.

May you be blessed while you read *Turkeyneck Hill and Beyond*.

Phyllis Dow Bex, Author

Contents

Creatures Great and Small

Two Heifers and a Tow Rope

Have you ever been in a predicament where you needed a tow, a push, or a shove? Have you ever been stuck or just broken down? Have you ever towed anyone, or pulled them with your car? What does that look like?

On the farm, we often used a tractor or a truck to pull another vehicle stuck in the mud or out of gas. We usually used a chain for towing on the farm. Therefore, towing another vehicle is common to me because of my childhood.

As a young adult, I drove my father-in-law's Chevy pickup towing my brother-in-law and his demolition derby car to the fairgrounds in Martinsville. We traveled about three miles from their home to the fairgrounds for the Morgan County Fair demolition derby. I was the only one available. My three elementary-aged daughters rode with me in the truck. We stood in the truck bed to watch Greg race, and guess what, he won first place. So afterward, I pulled him back home. That was an experience, especially in and around the crowds of fairgoers.

One year, my friend Georgiann decided to make a surprise visit from her home in Kentucky. She was returning a duffel bag from our Florida trip and was going to stick around to watch Super Bowl 2019. Her 1991 black Mustang didn't quite make it to my home.

After the four-way stop on Fairland Road, her clutch went out. She called me, "My car has lost its clutch, and I'm stuck alongside the road on the other side of the bridge. Can you help me?" Her AAA Plus card will tow up to 100 miles for free. I asked, "How many miles to your mechanic shop?" Georgiann replied, "Wouldn't you know it, it's 103 miles!"

While preparing to rescue her, I decided to visit the auto parts store to buy a tow rope. First, I checked the rear of my Honda CR-V to see if I there was a hook for a tow rope, and there was. In my seventy-year-old mind (at the time), I brainstormed an idea to tow her Mustang with my Honda back a few miles toward Interstate 74.

Upon arriving to this broken-down old heap of a treasure, I noticed a scared lady at the wheel. When she got out, her hands were shaking badly. I blurted out, "What is the matter with you?" The first thing she said, "I need to potty bad!" Then she said, "I've never done anything like this, and I'm scared to be towed! What if I mess up?" I just smiled and nodded, "It will be fine."

When I told her of my plan of how to tow, she really got nervous. We made a quick search to see if there was a place to attach the hook to the front of her car frame. There was, and I told her, "We need to back your car down this embankment." The look on her face was obvious she was not happy.

The Mustang had stopped near an asphalt lane going down from the main road. I instructed her to steer forward at an angle while I pushed the car manually on level ground. Then I pushed from the front going backward as she cut the wheel in the other direction. Gravity took over, and she was moving much faster. Georgianns' eyes were as big as saucers. I saw that she was frozen in time, so I yelled, "Hit the brake!" When she hit the brake, the Mustang skidded on the wet sand covered asphalt for ten yards. Now her whole sixty-seven year-old body was shaking as she exited the car. I didn't check to see if she wet her pants. Furthermore, she didn't much appreciate my laughter at the situation.

We attached the tow rope, and I pulled forward to tighten it. I called her cell phone so we could communicate. Off we went up and out of the lane onto the main road. Luckily, no traffic was coming our way. Truthfully, I didn't know if my Honda would tow that weight or not.

At the four-way stop, traffic was clear, so we didn't stop. My speed was up to 27 mph, and she was begging, "Slow down." In no time, the hook came loose from her Mustang. Georgiann hollered, "I'm unhooked, stop!"

We pulled over, and I attached the tow rope again. "Now stop going so fast!" Georgiann said in a very stern voice. "OK, but 27 mph isn't exactly breaking any speed record!" I replied. The simple truth is, I was so tickled I could hardly drive at all. Not long after, the tow rope came loose again. This time, she wrapped the rope around the front bumper and the frame. She put the hook over the rope and wedged it under the bumper. This held the rope until we arrived at the Fairland Fire Dept. parking lot.

Georgiann called AAA for a tow. They promised to arrive in ninety minutes. Keep in mind it took us over twenty minutes to move approximately five miles on a flat straight road.

As it were, nature kept calling her name. Now that the towing was over, we drove another two miles to the interstate and McDonald's. We celebrated with ice cream. You know everything is better with ice cream, right?

Thrilling Bull Rides and Cimarron Rose

During the 1950s while growing up on Turkeyneck Hill, we had a big herd of polled Hereford cattle. Of course we had swine herds of Duroc hogs too. But the best part about the old bulls was we could ride them, and they didn't care. Truthfully, the older they got, the more docile they became. In fact, it was common for us to hang around the barnyard where they were kept. Therefore, the bulls were used to us.

In case you wondered what the word *polled* meant, it simply means they were without horns. If I remember correctly, only the males had horns on some breeds of beef cattle.

So anyway, on lazy afternoons, I watched my brothers mount the back of an old bull in the barn. Most of the time, the bull just stood there. What's the fun in that? The one bull we all remember the most was named two initials, L D. In fact, Lois loved that bull so much she tattooed herself just above her right knee with his initials. At least that is what I thought until I realized L D was her initials also. As it turned out, the old bull's name was Low Dominion.

The old bull, L D, weighed over a ton, and he moved rather slowly. So, when we had city friends out to the farm, we showed them how brave we were to ride on his back. The bulls that riders mount in the rings are agitated to buck, but the commoner might not be aware of that little trick. It was a delight to be around the old gentle cattle. The young ones— not so much.

An old Hereford Bull, not our LD

In 1964, I was fifteen, and my friend Sandy was sixteen. We were buddies from the GAA club (Girls Athletic Association). One day after GAA, Sandy offered me a ride to my sister Clara's home. Clara and her husband Frank, with their four rambunctious children, lived in the country out on Mahalasville Road. Frank always enjoyed having a horse or pony around; not that they rode them much, but just in case.

One year he bought a beautiful Palomino horse named Cimarron Rose. She looked like Roy Rogers' horse, Trigger. Her coat was golden flax with a long white mane and tail. I never rode her but dreamed of galloping on her back with my long blonde hair waving in the breeze.

When Sandy saw the horse in the gated barn lot, she exclaimed, "What a beautiful horse! Can we take her for a ride?" Sandy was experienced with horses although she lived in town. Clara and family were not home, so I said, "Sure, but I don't know much about horses." "Don't worry, I know a lot about them," she said. "Do you know where the saddle and bridle are?"

I didn't know, but that didn't slow her desire. We found the bridle hanging on the fence post near the gate. "Do they have any carrots or apples?" she asked. I scurried to the house to check and came back with two carrots. "Perfect," Sandy assured me as she lured Cimarron Rose with the carrots and adorned her with the bridle.

I opened the gate, and the two came through to the lane. Once we steadied the huge horse to the wooden gate, we climbed up the gate onto her bare back. There we sat, all bright eyed, full of lofty expectations. Sandy began guiding Cimarron down the half-mile lane to the county road. It took forever because the horse was not interested in a trip down memory lane. Cimarron attempted to turn back toward the barn every couple of steps.

When we finally reached the road, Sandy warned me, "Hang on, this might be a fast run back to the barn." I stretched

A Palamino just like
Cimmaron Rose

around Sandy and grabbed two handfuls of white mane for safety. Sure enough, the horse jolted like a shot out of a cannon. I screamed, "Stop! Slow down! Do something!" But to no avail, the horse ran lickety split clear to the barn.

What took thirty minutes to get to the county road, only took two minutes to get back. Arriving in a full gallop, Cimarron Rose stopped abruptly at the gate. All the way to the barn I was dreading how the horse would dump us off her back. Surprisingly, we slid off and landed on our feet. What a thrill! Nevertheless, I never had the opportunity to do that again. I assure you, my dreams of long ago have at last come true. My flaxen long hair was blowing in the breeze just like I imagined.

Faux Furs and Faux Pets

Brace yourself, this is my opinion.

Living in the country on a farm was more than corn, soybeans, wheat, hay, and domesticated farm animals. When in season, we hunted wild animals like rabbits, squirrels, coyotes, raccoons, and deer. If there were muskrats in the creek causing problems, my dad would trap   them. If the ground hogs were a nuisance in the fields, we shot them. Of course, we trapped pests like mice, rats, as well as getting rid of barn swallows. We always had barn cats to control the mice population. This may seem like cruelty to city folks, but they had to be dealt with because they were pests who destroyed property.

Recently, I saw a report on TV that many high-end stores are selling clothing with faux fur. It could be merely a collar, a shawl, a jacket, or full-length faux fur coat. This allows animal lovers to have a fur coat that is both beautiful and warm without feeling sorry for the animal. Well, they just reported that they are not faux but real fur from animals. Imagine that! I laughed out loud at the thought of them being fooled. Many people who never braved a wilderness nor lived off the land have no clue as to the cycle of life in the country. All they know is their precious pets. We ate all but the pests and some of the young raccoons. Though raccoons were vegetarian, they were still pests and destroyed crops and kittens. They liked to eat corn. So as a trade, my dad enjoyed the hunt and then sold the furs. Again, that is what farmers do. Yes, they turn a profit everywhere they can. Furthermore, recycling things was done long before recycling was a green thing.

Keep your red paint in the can where it belongs, not on a fur coat that is being worn. That tells me that the persons objecting to killing animals for their fur pelts, recognize a real coat from a fake. Not so fast. The faux fur industry is getting so good at perfecting it that even the animals can't tell the difference. (I just made that up.)

Speaking of pets, it is a multi-billion-dollar business. I should have gotten into that business long ago, but instead, I chose insurance sales. I noticed there is pet insurance that people can purchase to cover the excessive costs of veterinarian bills for their ill pets. That is still an option.

It's wintertime, most of the time I am in Florida. One thing I have noticed is all the pets old people have in their possession. I live in a pet-free community. Well, that is a joke. It seems if they have an emotional support animal (ESA) certificate from their doctor, that is all it takes to walk through the pet-free regulation. However, what those of us who do not have a pet, or those allergic to pets, or those who do not want to deal with pets—must tolerate—is pets, even in a *pet-free* community.

It is amazing how the ESA owners go to the store, out to eat, to the beach, out on the town, and multiple places and leave their animal at home. Therefore, if they were really not just a pet, but truly providing emotional support, shouldn't they have them with them all the time? Hmm?

My issue with this is, why cause a fuss? Go find a place that is pet friendly. Why rock the boat? Why falsify your honest situation by getting a fake ESA? I can tell you why, some people are selfish and inconsiderate. Unfortunately, like a lot of situations in life, there are more people who look for loopholes rather than obeying the rules. After all, I speed every time I am behind the wheel. So, who am I to cast the first stone?

I love pets, I just don't want any. We had plenty on the farm, like dogs and cats plus the livestock. I love other people's pets. Heck fire, even two of my daughters have dogs in their homes and I love them. When I visit friends who own animals, I greet them. They are a part of their family.

Unfortunately, my daughter Kitte had a precious Maltese dog who suffered with cancer and had to be put down. I went with her to the vet for last rites and cried as much as she did. They are truly part of the family. A few years of mourning and now she has another little Maltese. My other daughter Katte has a Welsh Terrier, quite a comical dog. So, I do understand the love a pet provides for its master. The faux part is living in pet-free communities when they have pets and not emotional service animals.

Yes, farming on 450 acres with a lot of woods affords a wildlife refuge and hunting of many kinds. Our many cats and dogs were great pets, but they never traveled with us and always lived outdoors.

Pest Control Gone Batty

Life on the farm offered many opportunities to experience the life cycle of various animals. We ate plenty of meat, and thus, the life cycle of certain species was observed and well maintained.

Along with that, we could easily see the destruction caused by pests. My brothers George and Philip were in FFA. For those who don't know, FFA is a high school club for Future Farmers of America. It is an excellent program for young people to learn the methods of farming.

Every year, FFA sponsors a competition in the winter called the "Pest Eradication Contest (PEC)." Some would call it "a controlled kill," like deer population in state and national parks designed to thin the herd when it becomes too populated.

The participants of the PEC earn points for the various varmints bagged during the contest. Obvious pests are rats and mice. The sparrows, starlings, and pigeons who soiled up the barns must go. Moles need to be eradicated but I'm not sure how they trap moles in the winter. I was not in FFA. Once the pest had met their doom, the future farmer removed the bird heads, the mice and rat tails, and the moles' feet. The collection would go in a glass jar and stored in the freezer until the end of the competition. I always thought bats were included as pests, but I find no record of bats in my research.

Philip searched not only in our barns, but with permission, to the neighbors barns as well. He used a BB gun to shoot the birds perched in the rafters at night. I went along to help find them once they were shot. I always had a fun time with Philip, a kind-hearted brother. He always looked after me as his little sister.

George recalls how he captured many sparrows while they slept in the chicken house. There was a door between the roost area and the room where they fed and laid eggs. He said,

"I'd stand just past the doorway with a one-by-four piece of lumber about two foot long. Another boy went to the other side and spooked the sparrows. They came flying through the doorway. With my makeshift bat, I swatted them down harvesting about a dozen per swat." "That sounds a little barbaric to me," I told George. "His eye is on the sparrow, and I know he watches me." "God took his eyes off a lot of sparrows during the Pest Eradication Contest," George replied. Anyway, the contest helped farmers.

Speaking of bats? Did you know the Indiana Brown Bat is an endangered species? I hear INDOT hurried to cut forests of trees along St Rd 37 in Martinsville to prepare for I-69 when it was being built. The Indiana Bats' Spring migration is around April 1. The trees were downed before bats could nest in the trees. Bless their little hearts. You know, bats can be

The brown bat.

big pests if they get in your attic. You're allowed to get rid of the bats by simply encouraging them to leave your attic. Really? How does that work?

A few years ago, my pickleball friends moved into an existing home in Greenwood. Not long after they occupied the home, they heard noises in the attic. Ron went to the attic and saw droppings, but the precious little bats hid. The noise persisted. Next, Ron went on the roof to find a way into the attic. To his surprise, there was a large colony of bats living in their attic. A week later, the bats found their way into the house. His wife Deanna was going batty with them flying around in her bedroom. That night she slept downstairs away from the bats. As fate would have it, a bat found its way to her exposed leg and sunk its teeth into her shin. Yikes! Can you imagine Deanna's excitement? Tennis rackets became weapons as they attempted to rid the intruders. A few met their destiny.

While at the doctor with a dead bat in a baggie, she found out the history of the protected little feller. She promptly got shots preventing her from rabies. The doctor asked with a quizzical look, "How did this dead bat in the baggie die?" Deanna wisely and quickly said, "Suicide."

It was quite an expensive ordeal to rid the bats from their attic. Eventually, after hiring all the right people to administer the proper encouragement (exterminating), the bats left the premises and the attic was sealed.

Although it is a good thing to have bats who eat mosquitos, they need to stay in their own houses. Bats and other pests tend to commit suicide in many human homes and barns.

A colony of bats hanging in a cave.

Groundhog and Beaver Control

There are many pests to control on a farm. Some do insignificant damage, but some wreak havoc on a crop. Of the many wildlife, the groundhog is one who can destroy a soybean field. Well, this story is about a whole family of groundhogs who were having a daily feast on our soybean field in the creek bottom. Then there is the munching beavers that will be included later.

In the early 1950s, Dad noticed how the groundhogs were destroying the new soybeans and asked George and Philip, my brothers, "Could you boys find a way to get rid of them?" George was fourteen and Philip was eight years old. George decided to soak dried corn cobs in a bucket of gasoline. They had a bucket of gas and corn cobs, a baseball bat, and took them to the pasture where there were numerous groundhog holes. Burrowed holes are where groundhogs live.

For your information, the groundhog is also known as the woodchuck and is in the rodent family. How much wood could a woodchuck chuck? I am not sure—if they could chuck wood? They belong to the group known as marmots and are lowland creatures of North America. The groundhog plays an important role in maintaining healthy soil in woodlands and plains; as such, the species is considered a crucial habitat engineer. In the case of our soybean field, they were enjoying the bounty of fresh soybean plants. Groundhogs are intelligent animals, and capable of forming kinship with their young, understanding and communicating threats through whistling. They work cooperatively to solve tasks such as burrowing. Burrowing they did, in our pasture and the edge of the field. It was a torn-up mess with holes and burrows everywhere.

If you don't know the folklore of Groundhogs Day regarding getting rid of winter and having an early spring, the story goes like this. On February 2 each year, we watch to see as the groundhog rises from his den. If the sun is shining and he sees his shadow, we have only six more weeks of winter. If the groundhog does not see his shadow, well, we could be in for a late spring. That's how the legend was told. I have never kept track to see if it is true. After all, nobody really cares. We just look forward to spring.

Anyway, George had the bright idea to fetch water from the creek to pour down the burrowed holes. If that didn't arouse the groundhog, he'd throw one of the gas-soaked corn cobs in the hole and then pour a little gas trailing to it. Then they waited. Not all burrows had an entrance and exit hole. If the fumes of the gasoline didn't make them scurry out (only to be clobbered by the baseball bat), George lit the gas and ran. The soaked corn cob combusted into a small explosion. Afterward, the brothers moved on to the next hole. I asked him, "How did you know if you got them when it exploded?" He replied, "I didn't, but at least their hideaway was ruined."

This seemed cruel; nonetheless, that was their way of pests control. I know many people who call exterminators for groundhogs, raccoons, beavers, and squirrels, among others. Many types of vermin exist only to meet their waterloo if they are destroying property. However, that is the life of pest and their cyclical demise.

Moreover, in October 2023, I gazed out my back windows near the water and noticed my trees. They were all chewed up. They were stripped of any bark from the grass line up to almost four feet off the ground. The scratched-up bark and shavings on the ground looked like something was eating my trees. The most damaged were my two beautiful Bradford Pear trees. Seven trees in all had snacks removed from their bark. I panicked. I didn't know what caused the destruction. My guess—a beaver family had come to live near my back yard.

My trees chewed up by the beavers.

I called a friend who was a trapper for sport to come hither and check it out. Sure enough, it was a beaver family hosting midnight buffets. I didn't know we had beavers in our lake. As it were, this friend had a live trap he brought over to set.

The next morning, I checked the trap, and it looked like it had vanished. I told my friend, and he said he would come over later. Seemingly the trap did its job. He found the trap and caught a beaver. He reset the trap, and the next day, he caught the *big daddy* beaver. The third morning there was no beaver in the trap.   Apparen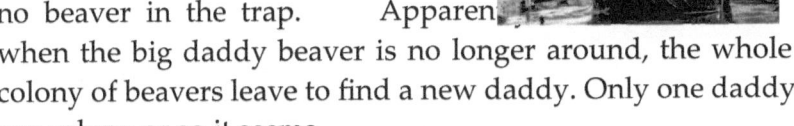when the big daddy beaver is no longer around, the whole colony of beavers leave to find a new daddy. Only one daddy per colony or so it seems.

My friend took the two beavers and who knows what happened to them, but they stopped munching on my trees. I struggled with how to treat my trees so they would flourish and not die. Luckily, my treatments were successful, as they all thrived beautifully the next spring and all summer.

Truthfully, there are all sorts of pests to deal with in our lives—not all have four legs. The best thing to do is face them and be done. And so shall it be with the groundhogs, the beavers, and all others. May they rest in peace.

Canadian Geese

Those who live near water, parks, or golf courses know all too well how much fun it is to have Canadian geese around. In my opinion, I think they are unwelcome squatters. The law protects them from us, and we are forced to endure their nuisances.

When I first moved into my home on a lake in June 2005, I was so delighted to watch the ducks and geese as they lived on the water near my shoreline. At first, there was a huge fountain beyond my office window overlooking the lake. I gazed out the window and was mesmerized by the fountain and the wildlife for hours. How serene, I thought, I was blessed with nature unfolding before my eyes in my own backyard.

As time passed, I realized the beautiful lake was not a lake but merely a retention pond built for storm-water runoff to prevent flooding. Those ponds are everywhere. Even so, the beauty of starring at water is soothing to my soul. I will call it a lake if I desire and at times I do.

At first I watched the mallard ducks as they fed in the shallow water. They dipped over to eat the grasses which grew near the water's edge. It was poetry in motion. Who knew they fed like that, not me.

In the heat of late summer, the ducks and geese found a resting place in my shaded backyard. To me, that was just icing on the cake. They picked my yard for lounging. How nice. During the fall migration period when the Canadian geese head south, I had a shocking surprise. While raking leaves I heard a loud noise. Turning toward the direction of the commotion, I saw the "V" formation. Coming in for a landing on the clear smooth water was at least a hundred honking geese. How majestic was their incoming flight and landing. As they floated atop the lake (pond), they squawked to each other for an extended time. My guess is they were relaying stories of their journey, complaining about the speed of each leader, exchanging recipes, and telling stories of what had happened all summer long. How extremely pleased I was that I was privileged to witness God's creatures in a way not afforded to most.

The peaceful and serene picture of nature in my backyard.

Isn't it funny how things change over time? Ducks gather near the pond longer than the geese each year. Every spring, the migration comes back in the way it left. However, now after several years of dealing with the geese, I have a totally different view.

First, let me give you the educational portion of this story. The male (gander) weighs up to fourteen pounds and his wingspan can be 72" and his body up to 43" in length. The female (goose) is built a little smaller yet visibly indistinguishable. The geese are primarily herbivores but will eat small insects. They live 10-24 years, but some have lived up to 31. Who knows and who is keeping track? At two years old, they mate for life and have their first goslings (hatchlings) in their third year. After migrating back to their birthplace in the spring, they breed and lay eggs. Though the female spends the most time on the nest, the male will also sit during the 24-

28 days of incubation. They usually hatch three to eight eggs each year. That adds to the overgrown population, bless their hearts.

The geese are usually a healthy bird but will suffer high mortality if infected by the H5Ni, the Avian bird flu. Geese are extremely aggressive while protecting the nest or their young. I found this out the hard way. They came hissing toward me leaning forward with their wings spread. It scared the heck out of me.

Because they can fly at an altitude of 3,000 to 29,000 feet, they are the second-most damaging birds of airplane strikes. You may remember the bird strike in New York when Captain Sully landed his plane on the Hudson River. My son-in-law pilot had a bird strike on his windshield while flying. A strike puts planes out of work for a while. FYI, the first bird airplane strikes were turkey vultures. Those are big birds as well.

Because of their filthiness and aggressiveness, the Canadian geese are supreme pests. Additionally, they have lost their magic in my eyes. They soil the water, our yards, sidewalks, golf courses, parks, and our landscaping. They nested and molted (lost flying feathers) in my flower beds. Then "hissed" at me and chased me when I went into my own backyard. A few times, they somehow lost their eggs and finally left my yard and their nest. I'm not saying I had anything to do with their eggs disappearing, but maybe. Therefore, I could carry on with my yard work.

Their nasty feces is everywhere. Geese eat two to three pounds of grass per day and deliver one to two pounds of feces. If you ask me, that is a lot of nonsense. More than humans ratio. I inquired about what I could do with these squatters. The best thing was to apply liquid bird repellent so they wouldn't find my grass yummy. I bought me a gallon and it doesn't work very well, but it helps.

Canadian geese hissing and squawking at an intruder.

Unfortunately, since the Canadian goose is here to stay, I'm getting a fence just as soon as I call the fence builder.

Lipstick on a Pig

Back in 2020 during the COVID pandemic, wearing masks and working from home caused a dip in the use of lipstick and makeup. I know I didn't wear much during the worst times of the pandemic. Currently with more people not wearing a mask, they are now back to using lipstick.

I wonder if anyone else thought about the lack of cosmetic sales during that worldwide coronavirus outbreak. I know it was on my mind. If we looked at the stock prices of Revlon and Cover Girl, it might tell a tale. When the mask usage eased up, those stocks might have been on sale.

Basically, we all know that *lipstick* is the cosmetic used to color lips. Everyone knows that. No one person invented it. In fact, it wasn't called lipstick until 1880. Upper class Mesopotamians used crushed semi-precious stones to color their lips. Egyptians made a red dye from iodine and bromine mannite. Cleopatra used crushed carmine beetles and ants to get the red color for her lips. Yuck. Who wants to kiss those lips?

It wasn't until 1884 that lipstick was manufactured commercially rather than homemade. About that time, they began selling lip cosmetics to their customers in Paris. By the late 1890s, the Sears and Roebuck catalog sold both lip and cheek rouge. Not until 1915 was the metal tube invented providing a portable lipstick for women to carry in their purse. James Mason Jr. patented the first swivel-up tube in 1923. Since then, the patent office has issued countless lipstick dispensers. Lipstick as we know today, evolved.

Max Factor invented lip gloss in the 1930s to use for movie actors. He used his other cosmetics as well and soon regular consumers were buying Max Factor products.

Recently there was a reel on Instagram with a little two-year-old girl who had lipstick all over her mouth. When inquired by her father, "Did you do anything in the bathroom?"

Little Girl: Uh-Uh

Dad: Nothing?

Little Girl: Mm - Mm.

Little Girl: I was putting some yip-ick on. And then getting my phone.

Dad: What'd you put on?

Little Girl: My yip-ick.

Dad: Who's was that?

Little Girl: It was my yip-ick pointing to herself.

Dad: Did you ask anybody if you could put it on?

Little Girl: I asked myself.

Dad: Did you see how it looked?

Little Girl: Yeah

Dad: "If you could describe it, what would you say?"

Little Girl: Like a noony-was.....her mom's...

Dad: So, who's lipstick is that?

Little Girl: Ah, Mine.

Dad: You bought it?

Little Girl: Yeah.

Dad: Where'd you buy it?

Little Girl: My yip-ick?

Dad: Yes"

Little Girl: I bought it at Homey Depot.

With that the dad lost control by laughing. Kids do and say the darndest things. And we love it.

However, due to the 2020 pandemic, cosmetics sales in general plummeted. Women were at home more, so why doll up? When going out, they wore a mask. No one could see their lips or most of their face. If they wore glasses or sunglasses, no makeup was needed at all. For many months in 2020, if people ventured out, they weren't out for long.

During the pandemic, the shiny makeup counter sales in department stores were down more than 40 percent. With a massive shift to *at-home* working, many ditched their makeup bags. Women simply were wearing less makeup.

In the early 2000s, the chairperson of Este'e Lauder coined the phrase, "lipstick index." This was a barometer showing consumer confidence during periods of economic turmoil. I'd say we had some economic turmoil. The lipstick index refers to the resiliency of cosmetics. Makeup was viewed as an affordable indulgence when high ticket items were out of reach. The lipstick index never saw COVID-19 coming. More than likely, lipstick sales were at an all-time low, with sales down more than 70 percent by the end of 2020. Yep, then was the time to buy stock, but we didn't.

Surprisingly enough, skincare product sales became the savior. With people mostly donning leisure wear at home, people started taking better care of their skin. Essential workers wore masks all day and showed challenges with their skin. Those workers needed new skincare regimens to correct their concerns. Some reports show skincare products sales were up over 234 percent. Therefore, instead of using the time to apply makeup back then, they took better care of their skin.

How about the Zoom calls or any video app to conduct meetings on your computer or iPad? Talk about a *wake-up* call. There we sat— feeling all comfy and cozy in our home office, then we saw ourselves on camera. Whoa! We're busted! It doesn't take long to see the blemishes and wrinkles that we never saw before. Suddenly, we rushed to fix our hair, apply a little concealer, and a touch of lipstick. There now, all better.

All online sales skyrocketed during the pandemic. It became a new way of life. (Guess what? Retired people are home all the time anyway, except for errands and lunch.) Those online sales continue. The biggest reason: people have learned the ease of ordering online. Most of the time their order is delivered free at their door. How easy is that to spend money and get your stuff too? Yeah, way too easy.

The brick-and-mortar stores came back slowly. Many didn't hang on during the shutdowns, and regrettably, most were the mom and pops. We appreciated those small hometown businesses.

Shoppers were soon able to shop for their cosmetics, to get their sample packets, try out the textures, and colors like before. Although, it took a while before retail stores were in full swing. They made it back and many changes were made. Even some of the big stores took a hit and closed their doors.

Going out to be with others is common again. Women are applying their makeup and lipstick like before. It is what we do. After all, why else do you need a girlfriend to go to the bathroom in multiples? We are touching up and trading makeup. Right?

The old expression, "You can't put lipstick on a pig," is true. We raised pigs on the farm without lipstick. But— the pandemic has taught us how important makeup is on a Zoom call. In the meantime, kids will still be kids trying on their mommies' *yip-ick*!

The Challenges
of
Growing Old

Dying on the Toilet

Surveys indicate the number one fear is public speaking. The fear of death follows closely as the second-worst fear.

As I mature, I believe a more distressing fright may be the fear of dying on the toilet. Can you imagine? I have a feeling if you asked enough people, you would find somebody who knew of someone dying while on the throne. In fact, many famous people did just that, but in respect of the deceased, I won't tell who.

While perusing my batch of emails the other day, I noticed one with a video titled "Don't die on the toilet." Please be forewarned at the frivolity of the email before I share it. This kind of humor is common for the over sixty crowd, and I suspect plenty of my audience resembles that group.

The video starts with an elderly man and woman sitting at their dining room table. The man says to her,

*"Did ya hear about Ralph, he passed away?" "How terrible,"
she replied. He continued, "He died on the toilet." "That's so
embarrassing!" she said. The scene cuts to the spokesperson,
and the sales pitch begins. "Dying on the toilet — every seniors
worst nightmare! You live a life of grace and honor only to pass
in the most humiliating way imaginable! Your rear end is up
in the air, your face is on the floor and a loaded toilet behind
you. Thankfully, there is a solution that is both elegant and
dignified: The Toilet Death Ejector.*

*"If you feel yourself dying, simply press the ejector button. You
will be ejected to your bed; the toilet automatically flushes and
releases a puff of lavender scent. Finally, a smart book falls from
the ceiling onto your chest implying wisdom. So, reclaim your
dignity and people will say, 'Did ya hear about Ralph? He died
in bed.' 'Oh, no!' 'Yes, at least he died peacefully in bed, reading*

the scriptures. The only problem, his pants were around his ankles.'"

Okay, so that goofy email is a bit ridiculous, but a little funny.

On December 31, 1988, I moved to Colorado for a sales management opportunity with Aflac. Little did I know of the debilitating recession out west. By April 1989, I moved back to Indiana. Before moving back, I contacted my real estate friend Debbie. She and another friend Barb sent me a video tape of a house to buy before I moved home. I liked the house and bought it sight unseen. I was amazed at the listing price of the house. Such a steal, it seemed, as it had been on the market for almost two years.

After the closing, I moved in the same day. I didn't get to preview the inside of the home until after I closed the deal. Hey, I was age forty then, what did I know? At the closing, they mentioned the elderly owner who passed away from a heart attack, and she had no close relatives nor heirs. How sad for her.

After a couple months, I got to know my neighbor Jeff. Arriving home from work one day, I walked out to get my mail. He is a bass fisher who competes in tournaments. As I walked back up my drive, I noticed Jeff casting with his fishing rod trying to hit a five-gallon bucket sitting in the middle of his yard.

It didn't matter that I had never met him before, still, I smarted off, "Catching any?" That was the start of a great friendship. Jeff and his wife Pam proved to be good friends for a long time.

As was their custom, they regularly dropped over for visits. I asked if they knew the lady who lived in my home before. He said, "Yes, I knew her well." Then he told me a story or two. The lady was eccentric to say the least. She mowed the yard on a riding mower with an aluminum pie pan tied like a hat on her head, "to keep the birds away," she said. Then other times she mowed without engaging the blade. Jeff later mowed it for her. Often she left mail in her mailbox for days. There would be thousands of dollars in dividend checks shoved in the box. Jeff said she had money and checks all over her home. Frequently, he took deposits to the bank for her. He saw the check amounts.

One day Jeff saw her mailbox so full the lid would not shut. He gathered the mail and went to her door. An awful odor radiated from the home. Since she didn't answer the door, he called the police. Sure enough, the poor soul *died on the toilet*. She was the perfect candidate for *The Toilet Death Ejector*. May she rest in peace.

The lady met her maker in the hall bathroom. When I told my teenaged girls the story, they felt uneasy. They asked, "Exactly where was she when she died?" Knowing the hall bath was their bathroom, the room next to it was the laundry room. So as any good mother would do to ease their fear, I fibbed, "The poor lady was in the laundry room." From then on, my daughter Jessica kept the laundry room door shut, especially at night. She didn't want the lady's spirit to come out and startle her when least expected.

Yes, as we age and our bodies wear out, we sure don't want to ever die in a compromising situation. May we all rest in peace when our time has expired.

Modern Conveniences

Appliances is an interesting word with more than one meaning. First, we find them in our kitchens, such as refrigerators and stoves. In my childhood kitchen, we only had an electric refrigerator and stove. Our only running water in the whole house was in the kitchen sink. That was it. However, an electrical fire burned down our home in 1956. The next home only had a refrigerator and water from a kitchen pump. The wood-burning cook stove didn't exactly meet the requirements or definition of an appliance.

I remember my mom using a wringing washing machine in the basement. In fact, when I left home at age nineteen, I don't remember having any other washing machine except the wringer. That appliance saved a lot of time and muscle while washing clothes instead of a washboard. After hot water was poured in the tub, we plugged in the machine and turned on the agitator. It was not automatic; we had to turn it off when we felt the clothes were clean.

Normally we started with white clothes. Often more than one load was washed in the same water before draining the tub and filling it again. We used a wooden stick of some sort to get the clothes out of the hot water and start them through the wringer.

A ringer washing machine like ours

The wringer consisted of two rollers situated on a moveable arm above the washing tub. The electric driven rollers are about fourteen inches in length and two-and-a-half inches in diameter. Evidently, the rollers are on springs because we fed the clothes through the rollers to squeeze the water out. It was important to keep your fingers and hands away from the rollers or you would be fed through the rollers. That would not end well.

There was another large tub filled with rinse water. Then we ran the clothes through the wringer again. Now we were ready to hang the clothes on the line outside. If it was brutally cold, we hung them on a line in the basement.

Do you remember when children got hurt and mom kissed the hurt and magically the hurt disappeared? As I have aged, I wonder, "Wouldn't we like our broken bodies to be kissed by someone to make them well again?" However, injuries and diseases don't work that way. The good news—due to the advancement of modern medicine and scientific research, we are not only living longer but healthier and more active as we age.

Gone are the days of accepting various pains and illnesses thus becoming a vegetable before its time. At age sixty-five, we have Medicare insurance! Yay! Have you noticed how many people wait until they are on Medicare to have surgeries? The over-sixty-five population have more surgeries for old parts which have been worn out for years. They may have been using brace, cane, crutches, walker, and other such devices (appliances) for locomotion. Hopefully, it isn't too late to regain their abilities once they have been "fixed."

You've seen the advertisement for the electric wheelchairs touting, "Not one red cent?" I'm guessing that means you can obtain wheelchairs or scooters for free with Medicare. I just saw an ad saying, "We have the worlds lightest mobility scooter" with an old codger holding the scooter above his head. I have seen a mobility scooter, and the occupant looks like they couldn't hold a loaf of bread over their head much less a scooter. After all, they have infirmities.

My friend in Morgantown was well into her eighties; she owned the perfect lift chair. She lived in an apartment connected to her son's home. This wonderful chair lifted her up to stand, reclined when she needed it, and laid her flat to sleep. Sounds good to me. One night she had it in she horizontal position to sleep. Unfortunately, a storm came through and knocked out the power.

When she awakened in the wee hours of the night, nature was calling. The lift chair remote did not work because the power was out. Furthermore, her phone was not nearby. She lay there for a few minutes deciding what to do. The urge continued. The poor soul tried to wiggle her way up, but she had neither the strength nor stamina to get herself up from the chair. Minutes passed and the need to be relieved was imminent. Eventually she did what any wise lady would do— a small blanket rolled up became her rescuer. When her son came in early the next morning, he was able to raise her out of the perfect lift chair.

In today's world, there is an appliance to fill about every need and every convenience in the home. So, live well and be glad you don't have to use a wringer washer.

The Pain of Knee Replacement

Do you know what they say? A minor procedure to some is a major surgery to others. Yes, they said that.

Knee replacement. If everyone has them, it can't be too difficult, right? After all, the doctor promised that recovery is a breeze. These doctors remind me of the group who deliver babies, yet they are men who know nothing about the true joy of labor. I am here to tell you this *breeze* is a lot of cock-a-doodle-do!

My personal experience with simple surgical procedures relates much like Murphy's Law. "Anything that can go wrong, will go wrong." Therefore, I enter any procedure with a fair amount of fear and trepidation. During times like these, I call on my gifted prayer warriors to go to work on my behalf. I thank God for them and pray for them to be blessed.

After twenty years of pain and three years of cortisone injections, the day arrived for my full knee replacement. Although, many friends and family have had replacements, this was my first. I hope it is my last.

As I reflect on my first childbirth experience, there are some secrets women just do not share with a first timer. My sister told me the pain felt during childbirth was a lot like a hard cramp during our monthly. I believe she didn't wish to spoil the surprise. Consequently, the first time I spoke with sister Lois after my twins were born, we had a talk. I'm not sure what her monthly cramps were, but pushing a seven pound baby through the birth canal was a whole lot more than a *hard cramp* during my monthly. For goodness' sake.

I've had two pregnancies/deliveries, five surgeries, along with many ERCP's and colonoscopy's. From my experience, I knew a thing or two of anesthesia and pain medications. Of course, everyone's pain tolerance varies with the individual and their age.

The knee replacement was unlike any surgery I had ever endured. Previous slice and dice experiences left me with most of my pain medications still in the bottle. To my surprise, I was not as tough as I usually am. Think about the process, my femur and tibia leg bones each had over three-eighths inches shaved off at the knee joints. The spurs and arthritis were cleaned and smoothed. Next, dental resin used for crowns were added to the chrome piece placed on each respective exposed bone. Then a silicone pad became my new meniscus, the thin fibrous cartilage at my knee.

Now before they stitch up the incision, all the ligaments, veins, arteries, need to be put back in position. What could be painful?

The best part was, a few hours after surgery, they got me up for a test drive to see if they got everything back in place. Imagine that? They break my leg, make it whole again, and get me up walking that quick. Modern science knows no limits. Easy peasy, right? Not so fast.

The anesthesiologist not only kept me asleep during the ninety-minute procedure, but he also woke me up. That was the part I liked the best. Yes, that's what I told them before they put me out. "Don't forget to wake me up."

However, the nerve block placed in my thigh to block the pain in my knee would have been better to have, lasted two weeks instead of two days. When that block wore off, oh momma! If I were a cussing woman, look out.

I am not sure who does this procedure, but a tourniquet is applied to my mid-thigh. We didn't need to have any bleeding out. The bruising from that was deep and the circumference was sore for weeks. This sounds reasonable, but for a thunder-thighed gal like me, pain was inevitable.

The promises of a better quality of life from corrective surgeries do come true after going through the paces. You know what they also say, no pain, no gain. I am happy to have the new knee. Just before the surgery, my doctor said he was getting proficient at right knees. What a relief.

Through it all, the pains of childbirth might be temporary, but the lasting joys of parenting are blessings which last forever. Hopefully, the new knee will be a blessing as well. Thank God for modern medicine and anesthesia.

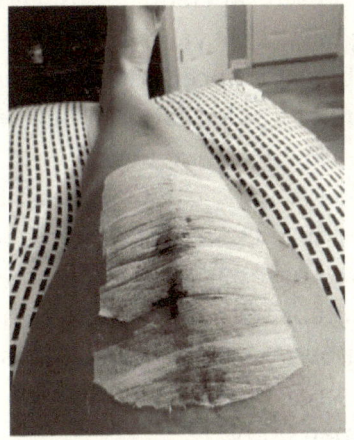 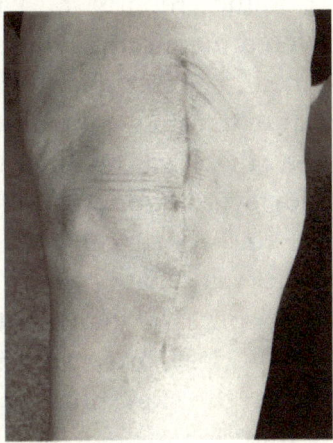

The knee right after the replacement   Weeks later after it had healed

Cancer and Politics

Is it possible some people haven't been touched by the disease of cancer in one way or another? Unfortunately, most families know all too well the pain of that dreaded disease.

What is the history of cancer and when was the first reported case? No one knows for sure. Researchers in the 1600s found reports of cancer in ancient Egypt. They discovered manuscripts dating back 2500 years before that. It contained a description of breast cancer, as well as a procedure to remove the tumors by cauterization. They went on to say there was no other treatment at that time.

However, Hippocrates (460 BC – 370 BC) described several kinds of cancer, referred to them as *karcinos*, a Greek word for crab. That is where we get the word carcinoma. He was describing the malignant tumor with its veins stretching out on all sides like a crab. Hippocrates only described visible tumors on the skin, nose, and breasts, as it was against the Greek tradition to open the human body.

Basically, a cancer cell is an abnormal cell which takes on a mutated form and multiplies. The cells spread primarily through the lymph node system and some move through the blood stream. When they attack certain areas and cause the good cells to decrease, that's when the trouble begins.

During the modern era of the sixteenth-eighteenth centuries it became more acceptable for doctors to perform autopsies. They revealed better insights into the cause of death. With the widespread use of the microscope in the eighteenth century, they discovered how the cancer cells spread through the lymph system. Poor hygiene affected surgery results, and many died due to infection. Once they began sterilizing their instruments and improved personal hygiene, the survival rates increased dramatically for all medical issues.

In the late nineteenth century, Marie Curie and her husband Pierre discovered radiation as an effective non-surgical cancer treatment. As it happened, Madame Curie died from an overexposure to radiation. Yet we thank her for her enthusiastic research which has saved millions of lives.

In 1955, Aflac (American Family Assurance Company) was formed by three brothers. John Amos, an attorney; his brother Bill, an accountant; and brother Paul who was an insurance salesman. In 1958 they introduced their first cancer policy to lift the financial burden for cancer patients and their families.

Starting in June of 1974, Aflac was listed on the NYSE as AFL. In October the same year, Aflac went international with Japan by selling the cancer policy. In the first year, Japan wrote over $25 million in premiums. All profits were repatriated to the United States. Yay, go Aflac. Ironically, our founder John Amos died of cancer in 1990. Because of his vision, Aflac currently has over 50 million policyholders and has over $128 billion in assets. I find it interesting that he had lots of money, and he developed a cancer policy. Yet, Mr. Amos still died of cancer at age sixty-six. Like the coronavirus, cancer doesn't care how much money we throw at it. People do survive to older ages and live in remission because of effective treatments. However, cancer is still the leading cause for medical bankruptcy.

The CDC states heart disease is the leading cause of death with cancer being second. Influenza and pneumonia are eighth. That score will probably change with the new and updated statistics relating to the 2020s coronavirus.

What I cannot understand is how it has taken centuries to combat cancer, heart disease, and a plethora of other ailments. Though improvements have been made, there simply are no cures, only treatments. We accept these facts unbiased. It amazes me how media of all sorts have politicized COVID-19.

Who is to blame, and whose fault is it that we don't have it contained? Folks, when the milk is spilled, we can't un-spill it. We can only clean it up as best we can. Do we need vaccines and effective therapeutics? Sure, we do.

Political affiliation will not make it happen any faster. There are millions of dollars already thrown toward research all over the world for this virus. I am glad that by now, it is not a death sentence to be diagnosed with COVID any longer.

However, can we mix science and politics? Is that how we produce answers to a life altering virus? I don't think so. I believe we should decide our politics on things which bring about good government and policy making for our land. Just like cancer has been with us for as long as we all can remember, political parties haven't changed cancer. I don't think politics will make the coronavirus go away either.

Now—go wash your hands, put on a mask, and confront the world with dignity. And "God Bless America."

Bathrooms and Disabilities

The things we never think of can and do happen to us if we live long enough. Being dependent on others during a surgical recovery can really humble a proud spirit. For example, did you think you would ever use one of those scooters to go shopping at the grocery or the hardware? I never did. What an eye-opening experience when I toddled around in Meijer and Menards in one of those carts. I had a knee replacement and needed to go shopping — for crying out loud!

It doesn't take long to figure out how to operate the scooter. The surprise is the reaction from other shoppers. I usually make eye contact with most people. However, they didn't look at me when I looked at them. They appeared to be totally annoyed by the person with the scooter. The scooter must have been in their way. I was careful and courteous but still got rude treatment from fellow customers.

That experience taught me to be much kinder to people with disabilities. I decided to look up the American Disabilities Laws. My oh my, we have come a long way, and it is for a worthy cause. Through advances in medicine, people are living longer. Therefore, we must make provisions for the disabled to manage as much as possible on their own. By doing so, their integrity and self-worth remains intact longer.

Another trick during a disability is using the bathroom. At home, I have a riser over my toilet. It is a portable potty without a pot, placed over the bathroom toilet. The handles on either side are like a captain's chair which enables me to push up with my arms to stand with ease. Sounds great? Using a public restroom is not so great.

I attended a gathering with "The Usual Suspects," a group of neighborhood friends from childhood held at Tomato Pie Joint in Paragon. Henry Burnett started this group several years ago. I live in Greenwood, about a forty-five-minute drive. Of course, I went to the bathroom at home prior to riding down with my sister Lois. After visiting with everyone for almost two hours and drinking three glasses of tea, I needed to make a pit stop before returning home.

For those of you who have had the pleasure of dining at Tomato Pie, you know facilities are basic. They have a one hole bathroom for all. It fills the requirement. The cramped tiny restroom makes it hard to get in and out much less to do what you came to do. This was my first visit to a public facility since my surgery.

In Paragon, IN. The Tomato Pie Pizza Joint

Another thing that happens when one is on pain pills, everything slows down. This is a bit personal, but I am usually one who spends no time at all taking care of any business in the restroom. So here I am in the bathroom at Tomato Pie. My cane is propped in the corner and the stool is all the way "down there." I don't sit on public stools anyway. The lid was left up by the "kind gentleman" ahead of me. I assumed the position, hanging onto the doorknob and the door casing. Then I realized that squatting caused great pain in my knee. But I did—for a long time. Remember, everything is slow. Suddenly, my legs are quivering, sweat is propelling out of my brow and rolls down the sides of my face as I wait. Finally, relief trickles out slowly and I'm finished.

While hovering in midair, *I had visions of me   fainting, falling on the floor, and the door not being able to open because I was in the way. I imagined they would need to take the door off its hinges to get me out of the bathroom. There I am, lying on the floor with my backside exposed. What a nightmare.* However, my worst fears were thwarted. I washed up and rejoined the party.

A week or two later, I joined friends for lunch at McAlister's Deli. Whatever I ate, wanted out. I was saying early goodbyes to go home to the comfort of my bathroom. Carol and Annetta insisted the restrooms there would accommodate my needs. As I went in, a lady was in the handicap stall changing her baby. She was taking her time by having peek-a-boo playtime with her child. Some people! At last, she exited, and I viewed the stall. The grab bars were perfect, the height was perfect, and a lid liner was available. Relief at last.

My lessons are learned. We must highly respect the ones who have the daily fight of disabilities whether they be permanent or short term. I thank God for my abilities and know I will soon regain all my strength. Bless you if you are one whose impairment is permanent.

Caskets, Newspapers, and Pogo Sticks

Do you know the difference between authoring a story and fixing dinner? Well, if you don't, you are in real trouble. Here is the similarity. When my young daughters were all at home, fixing dinner was easy. The hard part was creating the menu. It's the same thing when drafting a story. Once a subject is decided, then putting it on paper is a snap. So here we go.

As we age, we notice things we were oblivious to before. For example, the price of caskets and funerals. Who knows the costs of such things until you are in mourning? Nobody. People find cremations are not frowned upon as much as they once were. Therefore, many choose that method of respectfully laying the remains of loved ones to rest. By the way, do you know the difference between a casket and a coffin? Me neither. A casket is a beautiful resting place with padding and ornate fixtures decorating the exterior and interior where the deceased is laid. A coffin is a wooden box used still by the Amish and in old western movies. Now you know.

Though it all sounds morbid to speak of, it is an unpleasant fact when death occurs. For example, the price of a casket alone can be from $2,000 to as much as $10,000 or more. Whereas the lowest cost for a cremation is around $1,300. Of course, all the variations of each method will determine the end cost for a respectable home going. In the end, the living must decide what and how the deceased will be laid to rest. Technically, the business of caskets is a *dying* business. The cremains urns, boxes, and lockets are markets on the rise. This is something to think about. Truly, many of us do not want the *burden of planning* to be difficult for those who remain. For all, preplanning is a clever idea.

Another thing that's dying is newspapers. People around my age love the written word on paper. Especially the newspaper. Maybe the printed version of newsprint is on the decline; nevertheless, for us diehard folks, we prefer to hold the paper in our hands. We cut out pictures, captions, and articles for keepsakes. We enjoy sharing the paper with others when they come to visit. Many oldsters enjoy living in a community with a newspaper to read what's happening locally. Isn't that what we love about our local newspaper?

If you are like me, I read with a pen in hand. Underlining important points when reading a newspaper, a book, or any periodical that's important to me. Every Sunday at church, taking notes helps me pay attention. I underline scriptures and write messages in the margins of my Bible. Later when I reference that page, I see my scribbles.

There are some things we used to see all the time but are no longer around. Take the pogo stick for example. It is a stick with a place for your feet and handles at the top. The length of the pogo stick is about chest high. Underneath the footrests is a big spring around the stick. The idea is to stand on the stick and jump around while keeping your balance. That's all there was to it. My sister Clara had one of those for her kids. It was rather hard to keep our balance as we didn't have any solid surface to bounce on. We tried our best but the most we could do was about three bounces. The pogo stick has gone by the wayside except for maybe entertainers. They were popular when we had hoola-hoops and yo-yos. Occasionally, we still see hoola-hoops in exercise classes, the circus, and sometimes on silly reels.

As for yo-yos, those were all the rage back in high school. Kids brought them out at recess or after lunch and did tricks like, "walk the dog," "around the world," "over the falls," and "rock the baby."

A few years ago, George's grandson Daniel taught at the Tabernacle Christian School in Martinsville. He decided to form a yo-yo club. Daniel looked on YouTube and learned numerous tricks and fun ways to play with the yo-yo. Then he taught them to the club members. In fact, his and other schools met for competitions. Can you imagine that? One time at our family Christmas get-together, he did a little demonstration to show off his talent. Daniel felt it was another way for kids to gain confidence by doing yo-yo tricks. Now as a father of three, what a fun activity he can share with his children.

We never had a unicycle, but we knew kids who did. Again, this one-wheeled cycle was more for the circus than everyday kids to use. But where are they today? Who knows, maybe since most circuses have closed, there are no entertainers to ride them while they juggle.

Sure, many things of yesteryear have passed us by. However, there are new ways of dealing with life and entertaining ourselves. One thing has stayed the same, the age-old question will forever be—"What's for dinner?"

Controlling the Time or Weather

Do We Really Save Daylight?

I am old enough to remember when we had daylight saving time (DST) and when we didn't. Now we do again. Do you ever wonder where it all started and why? Me too.

Wikipedia is a useful source to find answers to questions, although not always correct ones. Either way, here are some answers. DST in the United States is the practice of setting clocks forward one hour during the warmer part of the year. Evenings will have more daylight and mornings will have less. Currently, all the United States observe DST except Arizona and Hawaii.

The Uniform Time Act of 1966 established the system throughout the United States. It starts the second Sunday of March and ends the first Sunday of November lasting thirty-four weeks.

In 1784, Benjamin Franklin proposed a form of daylight time. He authored an anonymous essay titled, "An economic project for diminishing the cost of light." It was written to the editor of *The Journal of Paris*. Supposedly, Parisians could save on candles by getting out of bed earlier in the morning thereby making use of the natural light.

Franklin calculated the total savings in Paris per year would be approximately $200 million in today's dollars. Nothing came of it as they thought it was a joke. Benjamin Franklin was ahead of his time on this and many other ideas. However, during WWI, as an economical method to conserve fuel, Germany began DST on May 1, 1916. The rest of Europe soon followed.

The Unites States adopted the Standard Time Act of March 19, 1918, starting the DST on March 31, 1918, to October 27, 1918. Congress abolished DST once the war ended, overriding President Woodrow Wilson's veto. During WWII, President Roosevelt instituted year-round DST, and he called it "War Time" until 1945 when the war ended. Many states still adopted a summer DST. From 1945 to 1966 there was no federal law concerning DST. Various localities could choose if they observed it and when.

In the 1964 Official Railroad Guide, twenty-one of the forty-eight contiguous states didn't use any DST. The lack of *time* consistency confused business and travel enough to push for the federal regulations. The result was the Uniform Time Act of 1966 as I mentioned above. Although it was mandated, states were allowed to exempt themselves. Yep, that's what Wikipedia said.

By 2005, the Energy Policy Act of 2005, DST was extended throughout the United States beginning in 2007. Now that it was in force throughout the country, the US Department of Energy required a study for the first-year results. Apparently, the report released in October 2008 concluded a nationwide electricity savings of 0.03 percent for 2007. What? Are you kidding me?

Additionally, in October 2008, a study by the National Bureau of Economics Research revealed the 2007 DST in Indiana increased energy consumption by needing more heat and cooling. It showed an increase of 2 percent to 4 percent because of DST. That percentage equals $1.7 to $5.5 million per year. Holy smokes! Before 2006, the Indiana counties near Louisville, Chicago, and Evansville were on time zones other than central Indiana. Currently a few counties near Evansville and Chicago are on Central time.

If you understand all of this and have followed along; well, aren't you special? For the life of me, I don't see the overall good reason to have any daylight saving time. But I'm not in charge.

In conclusion, have we saved any daylight? Don't we still have the same amount of daylight as we ever did? What about the clocks? If you are like me, you have multiple clocks in your home. Some of mine only show the correct time a few months of the year. I understand that many after-hours establishments appreciate the extra hour of sunlight to sell their goods and services. When the DST became a permanent fixture, business boomed like after-work golf and other outdoor activities. For the morning businesses, they just turn their lights on earlier.

Truthfully, we haven't really gained anything at all. We still have twenty-four hours a day. And we still have whatever sunlight we would have had if we had not changed the clock. As far as saving any daylight or time, I don't think so. Regardless, remember to change your clocks back one hour on that Saturday night when you go to bed. You don't want to be early or late for church on Sunday, do you?

Summer Heat and Cool Water

Summertime and the living is easy! At least that is the plan for most people. The scorching temperatures make most all desire cool air-conditioning. I remember as a kid, we had no air-conditioning in our home or vehicles. In fact, there was no cool air at school. When I went to beauty school, there was no air-conditioning in the old, four-story home on North Meridian Street in Indianapolis. When it was hot, we opened a window at home, in the car, or at school. We have become a people who rush from the cool car to the cool shelter. How sad that most indoor venues and restaurants are so cold that we carry a sweater with us in case we're freezing to death.

We are spoiled. We have become a high-maintenance bunch. Our ancestors lived without cool air pumped throughout their homes or in their *buckboards and buggies* when they were on their dusty trails. However, I am glad to embrace the progress of our modern age and do not desire to go back to the old ways of anything.

Modern conveniences that were once options have become standard. Think about it. To name a few; the garage door opener, garbage disposal, microwave oven, as well as air-conditioned homes used to be only for the rich. They were luxuries. Wall-to-wall carpet once was a selling point for a home. Now these simple conveniences are expected.

Last year when I purchased a new SUV, they wanted to sell me one with the "tail gate assist." This option allows one to wave their foot under the rear of the tailgate causing it to automatically open. The moment I get an option on anything, it becomes a "must have." I politely declined the lift-gate option. "What will come next, flying cars?"

As I continue to find places to cool off, one thing never changes, cooling off with a swim. At one time I was still recovering from knee replacement, I sought easier activities. Things with less stress and swelling later. That is a challenge.

While recovering, I missed playing golf, walking long distances, and of course, I missed my pickleball. Yet, I praise God I did very well and time healed the surgery. Now I can do most things with ease.

Friends in the Lazy River

A friend told me about the local swimming hole as an activity which allows me to be cool yet in the sun. The one near me has a "lazy river." A lazy river is a pool of water which winds around a large infinity path. Normally, people float on inner tubes on the rushing water in the circuit. The one I visit opens 9 a.m. to 11 a.m. for anyone wishing to exercise by "walking" in the swift waters of the lazy river. At 11 a.m., they release the inner tubes for floaters during regular swimming. That is also the time all the screaming and splashing children come into the pool.

The first time I walked the lazy river; I walked six laps. After finding out that eight laps was a mile, I freaked a little. Although I felt relatively well from the workout, I decided to take a nap that afternoon. Almost three hours later, I awakened. It must have worn me out.

I learned, speaking with my physical therapist, it is harmful to do too much exercise. He said that I should start with four laps for a few weeks and build from there. My recovery seems slow, but I sure don't want to do anything to impede my forward progress.

Another activity to fight the heat is visiting my friends who live on Sweetwater Lake. I can float in the water for a long time. Fortunately, the lake access has a gradual slope and is easy on my knees. The last time I visited, I forgot about the fifty steps down to the water from my car. It is the same number climbing up. What was I thinking? A modern convenience like an escalator would be nice. Down the stairs I went, one step at a time. The next morning after making the journey to the lake and back twice, I was sore. Both legs and arms had not been swimming or through anything so rigorous for a couple months. It was refreshing and just what the doctor ordered.

Through it all, cool air-conditioning and water therapy helps ease the heat of summer where the living is easy. We must remember to do what we can while we can still participate.

A view from their home.

Taking a dip in the cool water.

Superstitions and Friday the 13th

Luck is defined as, "Success or failure brought by chance rather than through one's own actions." There are people with numerous superstitions which coincide with luck whether it be good luck or bad luck.

Some think others have "all the luck" meaning they get good breaks in life. Others maintain they are lucky. I think I am lucky at many things. When looking for a parking spot, I positively believe there will be one for me right up front. That theory works well unless I am trying to park in the St. Francis Hospital parking lot.

A piece of research from Live Science on Google stated, "When our brains can't explain something, we make stuff up." That is how superstitions begin. You have heard of beginner's luck. That belief system has little stress. Beginners believe they will win, so they usually do.

"Find a penny pick it up, and all day long you'll have good luck." Anytime I find money I am lucky to bend over and pick it up.

Other superstitions are like *walking under a ladder*. Imagine a ladder leaning against the wall forming a triangle. The Christian belief is walking under or through the *tripod* breaks the Holy Trinity which was deemed as blasphemy to do that. Others thought walking under the ladder had a resemblance of medieval gallows where hangings took place. Perhaps we should stick with safety first thereby walking around the ladder, lest we cause an accident.

How about black cats crossing your path? The old belief is that witches took the form of domestic animals like cats, and they'd secretly cast a bad spell on you. The truth is Americans have more than eighty-one million cats as pets. Some are black, probably named Blackie.

Anyone ever carry a rabbits foot for luck, maybe on a keychain? Lucky? Not for the rabbit. He's running around on three feet. If you wear a cross with garlic tied around your neck, it keep vampires away. Why take a chance, right? More than likely, the garlic will keep everyone away.

Bad luck comes in threes, they say. When two things go wrong, look for the third. I always heard that death comes in threes, people looked for the other two when someone died. At my age, I've stopped doing that as it could be me.

A broken mirror gives seven years of bad luck. Frankly, I figured a broken mirror meant you had a mess to clean up. The belief was mirrors not only reflect your image but also reflects your soul as well. In fact, in the southern states of old when wakes were held at home, they'd cover the mirrors in the house lest their souls be trapped inside.

To counter the broken mirror hex of seven years, a shard of the broken mirror was taken to any tombstone to rub out the bad luck. Again, how long must one rub to rub it out?

It doesn't hurt to knock on wood, another superstition that keeps bad luck away. Good spirits are in trees, and the Holy Cross was made of wood.

Make a wish with a wishbone from a bird. The legend insists the wishbone brings the holder good fortune. When it is broken, the one with the larger piece has better luck. Bird bones have been used for decisive readings by soothsayers to predict the future.

Cross you fingers for good luck. Again, this goes back to early Christianity where two friends would cross their index fingers and make a wish. Now some cross their *hidden* fingers when they are telling a fib because otherwise they might tell an outright lie.

A few times every year, there is a Friday the 13th. That superstition began Friday, October 13, 1307. With France in deep debt, King Philip IV of France ordered a raid on the Knights Templar and essentially wiped them out. I'm guessing they wiped out the coffers to help their own debt situation. This event took place at the Temple Mount in Jerusalem with the grand master Frenchman, Jacques de Molay. Ninety percent of the Knights were non-combative, but the order was quite wealthy from managing charitable funds. They were overtaken.

Throughout history, Friday has always been considered an unlucky day. Jesus was crucified on a Friday. The number thirteen is an unlucky number. That's why tall buildings have no thirteenth floor. They go from the twelfth to the fourteenth floor. Wink, wink.

When anything bad happens on a Friday the 13th, it will forever be linked. For example, on Friday, August 13, 1956, our big farmhouse on Turkeyneck Hill burned to the ground. Even at the early age of seven, the date is imbedded in my mind.

According to a Phobia Institute in North Carolina about seventeen million people fear Friday the 13th. Fear motivates people to do strange things, such as I used to be afraid of the dark. I finally decided to face my fears and shut off the lights. Currently, I don't live by any superstitions as most of you don't either. Like most minor holidays, Friday the 13th is just another day.

Go in peace regardless of the number of the month or the day of the week.

Who are *They*?

Do you know what they say? It is amazing how often we use the *proverbial they* in everyday language. However, often we don't know who *they* are.

I found the definition of they in Merriam-Webster's dictionary. *They* go back to 1828, so it must be correct. First, the word they is a pronoun such as those people, animals, or things. Second, *they* — used to refer to people in a general way or to a group of people who are not specified. Third, *they* — can be seen as in a position of authority.

Now the use of singular pronouns they, them, themselves, or their dates to the 1300s. Forms of they are useful as a gender-neutral substitute for generic he or she, or any gender derivative.

Often we hear the following statements, and it leaves us wondering just *who* are these all-knowing people which affect our thoughts and lives? "What will *they* say?" "How will *they* know?" "What will *they* do?" "*They* call the wind Mariah." "*They* say it's your birthday." "*They*'re coming to take you away." "Who said?" "*They* said" and furthermore, "*they* didn't know what hit them."

In the news media of all forms, one hears *them* report what *they* said. I am certain when the report first began, someone was identified but soon became known as *they*. What does a listening and reading public do with all this reporting? For me, I like to fill in the blanks.

A friend of mine started going to an exercise class to lose weight and get in shape. After eight months of religious training, she greeted the custodian while leaving. Having her usual chat with the custodian, he said something interesting. "I've worked here for over twelve years and have watched the same people coming into workout each morning. I haven't noticed any of them losing any weight or looking fitter. Yet they keep coming in week after week. What are *they* thinking?

Don't *they* know to lose weight, *they* need to stop eating so much and stop eating wrong foods?" I think the dude was on to something.

It is strange that we never dreamed we would look like we do at this age. I remember as a young woman, I saw older people and thought to myself, "I will never look like them." Now I am them and wonder if I will ever be agile again. They say I will, but only if I work at it.

While spending time in Florida with friends, I am motivated to cling to my agility and youth as long as possible. Seriously, do they look in the mirror before they go to the pool? I didn't. My friends told me my bathing suit needs to go in the trash as it has stretched as far as it ever will. Arriving back at the condo, I checked it out in the mirror. They were right. It went in the trash.

Today's "trivia genius" reports about the United States presidential election of 1824. John Quincy Adams won neither the popular vote nor the Electoral College. Of the four candidates, none won the majority. So, how did he become president? I will tell you. It went to the House of Representatives, and they decided JQA was the best man for the job.

The going thing for car insurance these days are the *trackers*. They say the tracker will help to reduce my insurance premiums. I want to save money, so against all my friends' and family's advice, I signed up. Saving money sounds like a great idea to me. They sent me a monitor which sticks to the inside of my windshield. It is paired with my mobile phone via Bluetooth. In plain language, it must be connected to my phone wirelessly through the program called Bluetooth.

Every start and stop is recorded and measured by five attributes of my driving skills. Five ways of proving my worth for a discount; speeding, braking, cornering, accelerating, and of course, mobile phone usage. A star rating is recorded, and they calculate how much of a discount I receive annually. Currently, they have indicated my discount is a whopping $11.21. If my driving skills do not improve, they will get a nice Christmas present from me.

Proverbially, this is about all I have to say about *them*. You know what *they* say, he who laughs last, laughs best. Don't believe it. I was the first to laugh many times and never thought it was a contest about the best.

Above all, enjoy life like we used to on Turkeyneck Hill. Beware, if you have an Alexa-type device, *they* may be listening.

It Must Be Global Warming

Growing up in the country had its wonders. One of the biggest was we wondered how we survived. The reality of survival is a fine art. For example, when it got cold out, we'd throw another log on the fire. When it was scorching hot in the summer, we'd open the windows and turn on the oscillating fans. If we were hungry, we'd go to the cellar (basement) and fetch canned goods from the summer before. In the freezer we had meats and vegetables we packed when last harvested or butchered.

How about a new way of doing things? Many say new ways are better ways, some call it progress. Not so fast Einstein, new ways aren't always better. When you go out to eat, it's good, but is it as good as home cooking that your grandma and mothers could make? Never. Their foods usually weren't as processed nor filled with preservatives. However, going out is a lot less work—or is it?

Dining outside the home, some source of income must be earned to afford the price difference from buying groceries for home preparation. We fool ourselves thinking we'd rather work more hours away from home. Could it be we work more so we don't have to eat at home? Interesting concept. It has become a way of life.

During the year of pandemic, we found ourselves spending more time in the kitchen. I think many rediscovered hearty and delicious meals we could whip up with ease. However, habits are hard to break. Eventually, we all returned to the habit of going out to eat for the social aspect of being with others if nothing else.

Let's go back to the weather. One January, I spent a week in Florida. The plan was to stay longer but it was dreary, rainy, and cold. My thought was, "It is cold like this at home, I can go home and stay inside instead of paying for lodging here in chilly Florida." Now that I am home, I long for their kind of chilly weather. I should have stayed in Florida.

Has anyone ever explained *global warming* to you? No? Me either. I assume that is the process where the globe warms so much that it melts the icebergs, glaciers as well as the North and South Poles. I assume further the warming will cause oceans and seas to rise. Hence the water levels at the beach fronts increase and flood the shorelines. Do you suppose that is possible?

Another thing I hear— humans cause global warming. How can that be true? I know I am no scientific genius and never claim to be. But how is what we do going to alter the global temperature? Do we really have that much power? It could be I don't know how all the elements of atmosphere work together. I'll ask Al Gore the next time I see him. After all, he claims he invented the internet.

One thing for sure, this winter has truly been a tough one for everyone. I don't remember this much cold or snow for many years. I stayed inside for COVID and now staying indoors because it is too cold for man or beast. Frankly, I am grateful I don't have a beast. Then I'd have to take it outdoors to go potty. That alone is a deal breaker for having a dog.

The heavy snowfalls used to be such a highlight for all children when school was cancelled. Lucky for them if they were able to experience sledding down their favorite hills. We had some favorite hills as kids on the farm. The farm road which cut up the hill through the woods from the creek bottoms to the farm on top was a favorite hill of ours. This road is a north facing pass with many trees forming an arching canopy. Several inches of snow were needed to cover the arching trees as well as cover the tractor and wagon path.

I've told this highlight before of how some of us got an old piece of tin with the front end folded up and rode it down the hill when it snowed. It was a fast ride. The only way to guide it was to lean. Many times, we had to roll off that piece of tin or we could hit a tree. Walking back up the long hill usually generated enough body heat that we didn't notice the frigid temperatures.

Thankfully, those days of enjoying a romp in the snow have passed. I guess as we age, we find the finer things in life more enjoyable; like the comforts of a warm throw while watching Netflix or reading a book.

Yes, we learn to survive even if we do have subzero temperatures and a foot of snow. We can even call it global warming if you want. As for me, I'll stay indoors with a cup of hot chocolate and dream of my upcoming trip to warmer climates.

Can it Wait?

Yes, it *can* wait. Three little words, but they mean so much. If you can wait on a lot of things, you will be better off. If you save and not spend money foolishly, you might be very wealthy one day. Or at least better off than you expected. Many people *have not* because they waste money.

The problem with many people who *gotta have it and find a way to get the next best thing* all the time, is they never have enough. It seems enough is never enough for some people. Some are quiet about their expenditures, while others are like a peacock. They are showy. If only they could start believing, *I can wait,* and practice resisting indulgences, what a better world for them and their loved ones. Of course, retailers are counting on these big spenders to meet their quotas. Consumers consume; retailers are counting on it.

I do not consider myself a wealthy person, but I do consider myself to have had enough. Therefore, it is not a problem to share what I have with others. When I see a need, my mantra is— will I notice a dip in my bottom line if I help? The answer is almost always, *not at all*, so that's how I handle opportunities. Give it a try. Random acts of kindness work the same way.

However, there is a limit to my generosity. For example, we live in the land of opportunity, the greatest nation. Help wanted signs are everywhere. The workers are few, but the harvest is plenty. Often beggars stand along the roads, and most of the time I pray for them but rarely offer cash. A friend of mine has often seen them with a sign that read, *Hungry, Need Food.* She turned around and bought a bag of sandwiches for him. It turned out he wasn't hungry, and he wanted cash instead. Hmm?

I remember when my daughter Jessica was at Ball State. She was taking a full load of eighteen hours per semester, plus working a job waiting tables. While at home one Sunday, we attended church, and she heard of a children's ministry overseas. She was to send $21 per month to help these children. Jessica elected, on her own, to send $21 monthly and she did. I was proud of her for doing that. I am not sure how long she did; however, that has made all the difference. The simple act of giving regardless of how long you give it does something to your mentality. We know we have influence for someone else even if we don't know them.

In life most people are gathering and keeping primarily for themselves or their loved ones. That is all good, nothing wrong with that. Yes, we are called to a higher purpose, a purpose where we seek out to serve other people in small and large ways in addition to our loved ones. When we do, there is nothing compared with the good vibrations we have in our soul. That is what we are called to do as a Christ follower. So, we serve others.

It simply amazes me how much the times have changed and changed us. I remember back in the days when we lived on the farm, we had plenty, but we had nothing. Going to school was nice, but we had two or three outfits per year to wear to school. We had only one good pair of shoes. Our Aunt Bessie always bought us days-of-the-week underwear, so we had at least good underwear. However, we didn't know any better and yet, it was enough. If we wanted something, we'd have to wait.

No, we didn't want to live like that forever, but the practice didn't hurt us one bit. We lived with one television, one phone, no dishwasher, no disposal, no microwave, no thermostat, no air-conditioning in the home or car, no computer, no printer, no mobile phone, no clothes dryer, no hairdryer, no curling irons, no prepared foods (except for Chef-Boy-AR-Dee pizza mix on occasion). However, we didn't acquire those things all at once when we left home. Nope, it could wait.

Waiting taught us to spend time bearing one another's burdens, encouraging each other, being kind to others with hospitality and devotion. We were compassionate and spurred one another on toward virtuous deeds. We tried not to slander one another. We tried to be generous in all ways.

So, when you can wait to indulge yourself, just wait. It's an excellent, practical, and worthwhile characteristic to have. Plus, you will have enough stamina for the middle and the end of your life.

This rant was stimulated by so much of what we see in today's world. I fear the *now generation* will not be able to sustain themselves with their attitudes of pampering and not waiting for satisfactions. But for now, *can it wait?* — remains to be seen.

Let's Hit the Road

Elders on Vacation

Remember back in the olden days when we used to go places overnight? It wasn't such a big deal, was it? No, we packed our toothbrush and a change of clothes and off we went. Not much to worry about 35-45 years ago. That is unless we were high maintenance and most of us were not. But   away from home is a major ordeal.

If you remember the movie, *The Jerk*, the main character played by Steve Martin left home toward the end of the movie. There were lawsuits against him, and his wife deserted him. As he walked out of his mansion, he grabbed the paddle with the ball bound to it with a rubber band and said, "I don't need anything—except this, and that's all I need." Then he walked a little further and picked up something else adding, "plus this and that's all I need."

As aging adults, we tend to be like "The Jerk" only in a more precise way. It gets to the point when packing the car and someone asks me if they need one more thing, I always respond with a resounding "No." More often than not, it is the first thing needed on the trip.

That very thing happened recently when I stopped in Oak Ridge, TN, to pick up my friend Georgiann heading to Florida. She packs a lot of things—bags, hanging clothes, totes, and only one suitcase. She was quite proud of having *only one suitcase*. Then she asked if she should bring her jean jacket. Since I saw three other light jackets and a sweatshirt, and we were out of room, I said, "No." I was in trouble because she needed a heavier-weight jacket right away.

Being the big spender that I am, I told her I would buy her a jacket. So, I took her to Goodwill. She had never shopped in Goodwill. I informed her that is almost un-American. Yessiree, I spared no expense and purchased her a jacket at the Goodwill store. Bless my little heart.

There was a time when we all could sleep anywhere and slept through the night. Those days are a distant dream for most who are elderly. Now, it is considered a reason to celebrate if we get over four hours of sleep in one stretch. Furthermore, one must be cautious where they are on vacation and who they travel with.

What about the poor souls who snore? Snoring seems ok with them, but their traveling companions aren't as happy. Think about retreats like camping, fishing, shopping, golfing, and family vacations. There are always grumpy people in the mornings. Often, they are not the one who snore.

Perhaps a metamorphosis of some nature takes over our bodies as we age. Maybe our throats get flabby, and they turn into sound machines during our slumber. Nevertheless, I know people in their young twenties who snores.

Older people have much to consider when traveling. We must think carefully when packing. First, we need enough medications to last the duration of our absence. Then throw in some extra pills like ibuprofen, vitamins, senokot, etc.—just in case. Some people must take their own pillow. I don't get that, but it happens. Then if we have special equipment for our health, we take canes, walkers, wheelchairs, and the like. Some take oxygen machines.

A few years back I just about died in the night because I stopped breathing. That is usually how people die, I know, but this was scary. After a flurry of tests for my heart and lungs, they did a sleep study. Sure enough, I have sleep apnea. That is a condition when you stop breathing while sleeping. Consequently, the doctor prescribed a CPAP machine.

I take my little friend with me everywhere I go. Shortly after, I took a trip with my machine. My daughter Kitte came to pick me up at the airport. She loaded my luggage in the back of her SUV and gave my CPAP machine a sling. I busted out with, "Careful there, Kitte, that is my life support system."

As time passed, I learned to use it properly, and now I get a good sleep. Early on there were times I'd find the mask the next morning on the far side of the bedroom floor. How did it get there?

Since I am referred to as an "elderly person" on TV, I must consider several things before agreeing to a trip. The first thing to consider are my medications, do I have enough? The second thing, what are the sleeping arrangements? An especially important third factor, will I have access to an electrical outlet for my CPAP machine? Fourthly, I need to pack small, don't overload the suitcase.

Yes, growing older and traveling is not for sissies, it is for the robust at heart. Just plan ahead and you will have an enjoyable time while away from home. Even so, we should travel as much as we can—for tomorrow waits for no one.

Snowbirds Who Fly South

In 2005, my friend Diane moved to Clearwater, Florida. Since then, I have been visiting the area a couple of weeks per year. My youngest daughter, Jessica, moved to Florida in 2014 and then started selling real estate in 2018. Do you know what happens when a relative sells real estate in a vacation Mecca? That's right, I received listing emails every week. The longer she was in real estate, the more emails I received.

Every winter when I visited, I usually stayed for three weeks for the season. I chose to stay home in Indiana where my only granddaughter lives and to be near my other two daughters and family. Well, that is good in theory, but one of the two remaining daughters moved to Charleston and that sweet grand baby is a senior in high school with   lots of activities which keep her busy.

On Mother's Day 2022, my sweet daughter Jessica called from St. Petersburg to wish me happy Mother's Day and said, "Say Mom, did you see the most recent email listing I sent to you? I think you will love it, and it's up by Diane." Well, long story short, after a FaceTime visit to the condo, it was a done deal—except, I wanted my travel buddy Georgiann from Tennessee to go *halfsies* with me. She did, and we bought it without seeing it.

We made a few trips down to visit our new purchase in the summer and fall and are quite pleased with our decision and the whole community. On December 29, 2022, we arrived there for the winter and quite frankly, we think we are geniuses— especially when we see the winter weather in Indiana and Tennessee. To justify the expenses, we call it an *investment for our children's future*. In reality it is an adult playground. If people get bored here, it is their own fault.

With 2,400 different one-story ground-floor units, three pools and clubhouses full of activities of every kind, not a day goes by without seeing smiling faces. Golfers have three courses to choose from and pickleball is played every day. It is a true playground for the over 55 group. It is interesting to hear everyone's story of their careers and their *back home life*. Many have made Highland Lakes in Palm Harbor their only home after a few years of back and forth.

On the way down to Florida in December, we honestly thought the traffic was the worst ever. In the big cities, it felt like the locals decided to drive the interstates to clog up the highways. While traveling through Atlanta, we drove in the HOV lane. (High Occupancy Vehicle. The lane requires two people in the car.) That was helpful but not always fast. At one time there was a hearse driving next to us. We wondered, "If a hearse is transporting a body, does that qualify them to drive in the HOV lane?"

If anyone knows the answer to that question, please let me know. Upon arrival to our new home in the sunbelt, we crashed for a week. I honestly believe Christmas should not be celebrated at the end of the year. There is so much to do in December already, August would be a better time as there are no holidays in August.

One day we arrived home, and our garage-side neighbors were out. We had a nice chat. A couple of days later, an ambulance was backing into our shared driveway. That neighbor had fallen, and he had to be taken to the hospital. With the average age being seventy, we see many ambulances every day in this community. He was hospitalized for a couple of weeks. The wife is fit-to-be-tied and ready to return to Iowa. "Iowa? I wouldn't go to Iowa for the winter!" I thought to myself.

After having been here for weeks, it seems like this whole neighborhood of older folks is a perfect storm for emergency medical attention. It seems everyone is just one fall away from quick ride in an emergency vehicle. Not a day goes by, that ambulances and fire trucks go by our condo. We see many people walking on the sidewalks with their walkers and canes. Or their appliances are near the entry to the pools. It is a good thing that they can get out.

We have nicknamed the state of Florida— "Heavens waiting room." Just in case, I have a stack of my daughter Jessica's business cards for people needing a realtor to sell their condo. I know I am fortunate to be here. One never knows when their time will come to be confined or worse. Many people don't get the chance to leave the wintry weather for a warmer climate. We all know if we stop moving, well, we will assuredly stop moving.

So, here's to all of you in the northern and cold climates who can't be here in the southern states, I will exercise a lot and think of you while I am here. I hope that helps.

Don't Forget Your Meds

It can be frustrating when traveling and we run out of our maintenance drugs. It happens. Sometimes we've been delayed and have not taken enough prescriptions for emergencies. Rest assured; we are in good company.

As we age, our bodies become more dependent on medications to maintain good health, or better health at least. It frustrates many people to take meds. Not too long ago, my first prescription was for acid reflux. I knew early in the day if I'd forgotten it. While visiting my doctor, the nurse asked me if I was taking my medication as directed. When I told her, "No," she said, "Do you have a cell phone?" Yes. "Then set the alarm to take your meds every morning." I did and it worked most of the time. In fact, I put a second alarm on it that read, "I mean it! Take your meds!" Now I have three other pills, so it is important to keep this well-oiled machine of mine in tip-top shape.

One spring my sister Carol, her husband Jim, along with Georgiann and I went from Clearwater across the state of Florida to Vero Beach. Our niece Debbie drove over from Arcadia as well. Sister Lois and her husband Dick were staying at Vero Beach in an exceptionally large house. They invited us for an overnight stay and to visit the area. We toured the sites, shopped, saw the

Playing cards with Lois, Carol, and Georgiann at the Vero Beach home.

Atlantic, ate delicious food, watched college basketball, and played cards. Of course, we had a wonderful time.

Before bed we huddled together to take our *night pills*, and Carol discovered she forgot her days-of-the-week pill holder. No fear, we don't need to worry if we forget our medications while traveling with this bunch. We are relatives with similar DNA. I gave Carol a rosuvastatin, Lois gave her a Co-Q 10 and a calcium tablet, Jim gave her a metformin, and Georgiann gave her a Zyrtec. Whew, problem solved. Now for the morning medicine rituals.

Brother George uses an old match box with a rubber band to carry his noon pills in his pocket.

I heard someone say, "Guard your youthfulness like someone was trying to break in and steal it." I wondered what they meant by youth. They probably meant our looks, our shape, our buoyancy, and mostly our attitudes. A person with a youthful spirit remains young beyond their years. Maybe it has a lot to do with smiling and eye contact. Guarding your ability to move and be active is important.

At times, just getting out of a chair or from your automobile is a challenge. After that, the first few steps might be a little tricky. At a restaurant, I have learned to stand up and then gather my things for a moment. I continue the conversation while standing there until my feet and legs get awake enough for me not to look like a cripple when I march toward the door.

I have noticed that as we mature, we lose our filter when we converse. Perhaps we may be tired of caring, or we can't remember an intelligent reply—so we merely speak our mind. During a gathering at my home, one gal spoke of getting up at 6:00 a.m. because she enjoys the mornings. My friend Daphna replied, "No retiree should ever get up at 6:00 a.m. unless they have a cow to milk." There might be some truth in that. In Florida while waiting with friends, a slow poke friend was last to arrive. When they appeared, one of them said,

"I've whitened my teeth and put on shoes for you, now you make me wait?" See—no filter.

Let's talk about all the new road construction. What puzzles me are the roundabouts. Just when I think I'm one of the *cool kids,* and I can maneuver in my lane on a roundabout, I have taken the wrong road. Now I must turn around, go back, and find the correct road. To myself I judged them, "Why don't they put up a road sign?" When I got back to this roundabout, there was a huge sign pointing to my path. I thought, "Wow, that was fast, that sign wasn't there a minute ago."

The new interstate changes have the new *tear drop* systems instead of a perfect circle like a roundabout. It doesn't allow you to go around; you either turn at one of the two or three opportunities or just keep going on the same road. How about those odd-ball interchanges that put you on the opposite side of the road and then you have a stop light at either side of the bridge. Crazy, I tell you. Who thinks of this stuff?

Being a forgetful elderly person who enjoys retirement is not for the faint of heart. No, there are a lot of assumptions to which we must submit. Like: remember your meds while traveling, taking care of yourself, and staying alert-- especially while driving on roundabouts.

Carol carries pills in this little Tupperware for her purse.

Wind Turbines on the Road to Chicago

Recently, my adult children vacationed in Europe. Before their trip, they had the bright idea to enroll in the Trusted Traveler Program for Global Entry. The short story to all that? When one travels, they go to the short line while going through customs, and other help. I need one for my upcoming trip abroad, I decided.

After applying online, Customs and Border Protection require a face-to-face interview. They are available only at certain airports or processing centers. The nearest one with an opening for an interview before my trip was located at the Chicago O'Hara airport. Driving to O'Hara and conducting the interview was uneventful. The actual interview lasted less than five minutes. However, the heavy traffic on the drive home plus rainstorms kept me on the road longer than expected. Many flights will be required to recover the eleven hour round trip. The time I was supposed to be saving by having this "pass" has already been spent. I have five years to find out if it was worth it before renewal.

Intriguingly, it has been a while since I have traveled on Interstate 65 from Indianapolis to Chicago. To my surprise, the fields are full of "wind turbines" for miles. They stood majestically spinning on both sides of the interstate. What a remarkable sight! As a youngster growing up on the farm, we called them windmills. Our windmill provided power to pump the water up from the well into a holding tank. This demonstrated how powerful the wind can be if it is harnessed properly. The sheer volume of these wind turbines on Interstate 65 caused me to ponder, how exactly do they work? I found the research interesting. First of all, if I wanted a personal one, I'd need $10-$14,000. Yikes! I will keep Duke Energy for my power.

The wind turbines along Interstate 65 in northern Indiana

Here are a few pros and cons of having wind as a power source of energy. They say it is renewable, free, clean, and wind has no emissions. It cannot be stored. However, the wind only blows seventy-five percent of the time, so placement is strategic. The other twenty-five percent, coal or gas sources assists the turn. Supposedly, the EPA offers kickbacks for wind and solar electricity.

The turbine must face the wind for the blades to turn. Wind turbines are expensive to build. The wind-driven source is approximately one percent of the electric consumption around the world. Each of the three turbine blades is 178-195 feet long. The tower is 264-413 feet high. They are monsters. Though it looks as if they are barely moving, they rotate many revolutions per minute at speeds from 7 to 56 mph. The 60-meter blade is made of light-resistant material and will automatically stop if they are spinning too fast. This protects against storms and high winds.

The turbine needs seven to twelve revolutions per minute to produce electricity. The function of the gear box is to convert the turning speed by X100 into the generator. Now the generator converts this kinetic energy making it easier to transport and use. Electricity in the generator as direct current is conducted down the tower to the base of the wind turbine into a transformer. From the turbine transformer, the alternating current is transferred by underground cable to a substation. Here the voltage is increased again to feed the power grid/power lines for use by the end user. Sounds simple and easy to follow. Well, if you didn't get it, you are not alone.

The biggest problem with the windmill/turbine is they are not consistent. They are built on an axis to follow the wind. Many have weathervanes to tell the turbine which way to turn into the wind if there is any.

The farmers in the northwestern part of Indiana are on to something. That is the windiest part of the state. In 2008, companies first offered to place wind turbines on their farms. At first, the farmers resisted as each turbine requires one acre. They must be one thousand feet from the edge of their property line and from the next turbine. Wind turbine contracts are twenty to twenty-five years long. The good news is they can earn $6 - $8,000 per year per wind turbine. Not bad for leasing a one-acre plot? Sadly, a quarter of a million birds die annually from wind turbines. But domestic cats kill 2.4 billion birds every year. Therefore, you need to think about that if you're a bird lover.

For safety sake, red lights flash in sync at the top of the wind turbine to keep the air traffic away during the dark hours. Hopefully, they won't mistake them for a runway.

Now you know more about wind turbine electricity than you ever wanted. Guess what? You'll never get this five minutes back. At least you didn't spend eleven hours to save one hour going through customs and passport control like I did. However, it was the experience of getting the global entry that makes all the difference. In life, we evolve with our experiences.

Goldilocks Weather

Ah, fall is finally here! I knew it would show up, it always does. Fall is my favorite season of the calendar. The air is cool, the sun still shines, and the ground is firm. Open the windows and doors and let the cool breeze flow inside. Yes, it's the fragrance of heaven.

Most mornings as I was waking up, I turned on the TV weatherman— Chuck Loften. You know, those meteorologists report the weather, and they are rarely correct. I ask you this, "What other profession can employees be wrong the majority of the time and still keep their job?" I give up. But the meteorologist can. They love a good storm. Have you watched their reaction to hazardous storms? Their adrenaline is pumping more than any other time.

This particular morning, he promised, "Folks, it's going to be another beautiful autumn day out there. These cooler temperatures are only getting up to the low 70s with plenty of sunshine. I call this 'Goldilocks weather.' It's not too hot, not too cold—it's just right." I chuckled to myself and thought, "Yes, Chuck, good old Goldilocks."

This year we have had some beautiful days in the last several weeks. The trouble is, we have had virtually no rain. All our fields and yards are parched. Even those people who have a sprinkler system for their lawns have dry brown grass. Hopefully, we will get substantial rainwater soon. Another friend who was visiting from out of town suggested that these beautiful days should be called "Chamber of Commerce" days. That is when businesses and other buyers visit our town to decide if a new plant or store should be in the area. Let's face it, sunshine and mild temperatures always make us dream, "Gee whiz, this is a nice place, I think I could live, shop, or work here."

In the spring of 1969, I remember when my husband was interviewing for several job offers. He was finishing his studies at Purdue. On one occasion, we flew to Baltimore. We roamed the area after his interview. It rained the entire weekend of our stay. Although he had a sweet offer, he didn't take it because our opinion of Baltimore was awful. I haven't been back since. They needed some "Goldilocks weather" or a "Chamber of Commerce" day or two when we were there, and we might have landed there instead of Pittsburgh.

When my daughter Jessica and I went to Denver to interview for a position with Aflac, we thought we had died and gone to heaven. It was early December with a lot of fresh powdery snow, bright sunshine, and the beautiful Rocky Mountains as a backdrop. After the interview, we spent the next two days skiing at Breckenridge. Oh my, the weather took us for a ride down Goldilocks Lane for sure. It was *just right*. As it turned out, the position I took was great, and the outdoor activities were the best. Someone forgot to tell me about their economy. Colorado had a major recession in 1989. Beautiful weather and scenery don't buy insurance, people with jobs do. I had never witnessed so many empty buildings and major roads in disrepair as I did when we lived in Denver for those few months. We moved back to Indiana after the ski season was about over. Of course, it was a Goldilocks Day when we moved back home to our Hoosier welcome.

How about outdoor venues? We always need pleasant weather for those occasions. Brides imagine perfect weather for their weddings. Who doesn't? I remember my wedding was held in Goldilocks weather. In fact, I don't remember any harsh weather for all the weddings I have ever attended.

Many activities like weddings, family reunions, parties, and hundreds of festivals were canceled when we had the COVID-19 pandemic. We weren't faint of heart; we knew those activities would return in the future.

The truth is we can never control the weather. We plan a picnic or parade and hope for the best. It is better that we don't allow the weather to be a scale for our mood. I usually do not allow the weather to be my barometer for a good mood. However, I don't love frigid freezing weather at all. I just stay home when that happens.

When my granddaughter Maisy was in pre-school, I picked her up one day. I asked Maisy about her day, and she replied, "You get what you get, and you can't throw a fit." "What was that for?" I asked. "That is what I learned today," she said with authority. Maybe we should remember that little quip when it is freezing cold, damp, and gray this winter.

However, most of us do have a little bounce in our step when it's a Chamber of Commerce Day or Goldilocks weather. When it is fall, it seems a must to pick apples at an orchard and perhaps make a pumpkin pie. Roasting marshmallows over an open fire sounds good too. Enjoy your fall, or whatever is your favorite season. Keep in mind that a new season is just around the corner, and the current weather won't last long.

The Traffic Doesn't Care

Have you noticed—the bigger the hurry, the slower the traffic? The sorry truth is the traffic doesn't care about your pressing appointment. As my sister Lois always exclaims, "Get off my tail— you should have left sooner."

We all know how that goes. Yes, we should leave sooner, but we don't always do that, do we? The last-minute quick phone call can turn a short call into a long one. What about when life runs amuck, which causes delay? Situations like, the dog got out, your clothes weren't dry, the food burned, and needs to be cleaned up, or the kids made a mess. People can't find their keys, their belt, their wallet, or their glasses. "Hold the presses, I can't find my phone." The list is endless.

Of course, we all know there are 24 hours or 1,440 minutes in each day. Everyone has the same amount of time. It seems some people manage their time better than others. Time management is a learned art. We'd all be more efficient if we took the time to plan. We think we do, but we don't always plan.

Do you ever speed? The more accurate question might be, do you ever drive the speed limit? Most people tend to go over the speed limit even when they are not in a hurry. Unfortunately, I am one of those people.

When my twins were in kindergarten and my little Jessica was home with me, I was caught in a speed trap. It was the first time I had ever been stopped by the police. This is back to before we were required to put our three-year-olds in a five-point harness child seat. Jessica was *standing* in the front bench seat with me. When I pulled the car to the side of the road she asked, "Where are we going?" I replied, "There is a police car behind us."

About that time, he approached my opened window. With a quivering lower lip she inquired, "Are we going to go to jail?" I assured my Jessi, "No, we aren't going to jail, but I might have to pay money for going too fast." Sure enough, I got my first traffic ticket for speeding. I was a slow learner as I've received many speeding tickets since.

When on any interstate, and you only travel at the speed limit you become a menace to the traffic flow. In fact, other drivers may even honk their horns at you. Some drivers are so helpful at times they simply *point* the way you should go with a hand gesture. Consequently, it is normal to speed up. Thank God for cruise control because often people daydream or are on the phone and forget to keep up with the flow, or worse yet, they drive too fast.

My friend's son and his friends did a study several years ago. One Saturday the kids drove six cars around Indianapolis on Interstate 465. Their intent was to see what would happen if two sets of three cars next to each other all traveled at the speed limit in all three lanes. The second set of three served as a buffer for the first three.

As you may imagine, it caused a massive backlog by the time they made the complete loop. Fortunately, they got off 465 unscathed. They did notice a lot of horn honking and finger waves. However, their findings were complete. For the traffic to flow freely, interstate travel must have various speeds.

You may have noticed when traveling a long distance, there are always a few cars who travel with you. When traveling at the same speeds, they become your travel buddy. On a long trip, you notice crazy drivers too. Stay away from those people who just can't pick a lane. Any lane would do, just pick one. You know those people are not running on all cylinders.

The definition of "traffic" was originally applied to road travel. Trafficking has expanded to moving illegal drugs or merchandise, people, and of course data. They are all a concern for us. The cyber trafficking is the most sophisticated of all traffic. The chips inside all our devices and electronics are listened to by computers and will key in if it detects certain protocols.

I understand the desire of many people who go 'off the grid' to the backwoods where there is no traffic of any sort except maybe wildlife. That life is nice for a week or two, but I am way too social for surviving in the backwoods permanently. We've had enough isolation with various illnesses and the winter weather.

How ever you envision traffic, if you drive, you will find pesky traffic. Even if you plan purposefully and carefully, you could still find yourself stuck in traffic. No one can predict accidents, floods, downed trees, a herd of animals, ice, and snow. The slowdowns happen.

Just know that when you get upset and crazy and want to exercise road rage on some fool who is messing with your good travel time—the traffic truly does not care.

Twenty Minutes

What can happen in twenty minutes? Evidently a lot of things can.

Lois's daughter Kris, used to live in Chagrin Falls, Ohio, a suburb of Cleveland. One weekend in 1998 my sister Lois, my daughter Katte, and I paid her a visit. If I remember correctly, Kris was having a shower expecting her first birth, Eric. It was a nice drive over and wonderful to visit the area. Kris made her home in beautiful Chagrin Falls ever since she graduated from college in 1988.

The village was established and incorporated in 1844. It covers parts of three townships in two counties southeast of Cleveland. In the 2010 census, the village population was 4,113. Going directly through downtown is the Chagrin River that includes a natural waterfall. I remember seeing the little storefronts and shops along the red brick street of the main drag. There is a large white gazebo near the bridge and the falls.

In 1992, Kris and her then boyfriend Brant stopped at the gazebo after a short twenty-minute bike ride. That is where he proposed marriage to Kris and presented her with a ring. Isn't that a sweet fairy tale story? Well, it is true, it really did happen. They are still married today, must be true love.

Back to while we were visiting with them in 1998, we wanted to go to dinner someplace unique. Kris and Brant suggested various places. I asked, "How far away is that?" Brant replied, "Twenty minutes." Then another restaurant was suggested. Again, I asked, "How far?" Brant's reply was the same, "Twenty minutes." Then Lois suggested an authentic Italian restaurant in the Italian district of Cleveland. I said to Brant, "I suppose this restaurant is twenty minutes away as well?" He said, "Yep, twenty minutes." It was a geographical and mathematical anomaly, all twenty minutes away.

The five of us piled up in the car and Brant drove to the restaurant. After we had been driving for about twenty minutes I asked the dreaded question, "Are we almost there?" Of course, Brant smiled and said, "Twenty minutes." Needless to say, it was a tad longer than twenty minutes.

After Brant put our name on the wait list, he rejoined the women. We said, "Don't tell us, let us guess, it will be twenty minutes?" Smilingly he said, "Correct." Apparently being in Cleveland was a twenty-minute numerical miracle! We are always only twenty minutes from anything.

When the server took our order and she said, "We are a little slammed tonight, it might be twenty minutes before your food order is ready." Of course, we laughed and knew that was coming. The food came, we ate and guess what—we were twenty minutes back home to their house.

So, with that in mind, I have used it on a few occasions. For example, I live off State Road 135 in Greenwood. I tell everyone that I am twenty minutes from the circle in downtown Indy. From my home to Martinsville, it used to take twenty-five minutes. But once the interstate is finished, it will be more like twenty minutes. I can't wait.

People who travel on 37 between Martinsville and interstate 465 are truly looking forward to the completion of that stretch of road. Progress is nice once it is completed but the growing pains to get there is difficult.

Thinking about twenty minutes, most meals are prepared within a twenty-minute time limit. When a seasoned cook is in the kitchen, most breakfasts, lunches, and dinners can be completed within twenty minutes. Now if you are frying chicken, preparing a roast or anything requiring more time, more time is needed.

Speaking of which, I prepared a fried chicken dinner for a Sunday lunch for my twins' birthday. That is one of their favorite meals. Kitte, who had not mastered the skill of frying chicken, wanted to help me so she could learn. It was nice to have help in the kitchen. After we finished frying chicken, I made the gravy too. Kitte said, "I can make all of this." I assured her, "Yes, it isn't magic or difficult, it is labor or love, because it takes a couple hours."

However, once we sat down to eat the fried chicken, mashed potatoes, gravy, corn, green beans, and deviled egg; we were finished-- in twenty minutes. So, when you are facing a challenge whether it be fun or difficult, please enjoy. As you may know, it could all be over in twenty minutes.

A Vacation Genius

Frosty winter days make us wish for warmer climates. Our early winter had been mild in central Indiana leading up to our departure. Of course, no one can accurately predict the weather, not even the meteorologists. I have often wondered how much training it takes to become a meteorologist. They always get paid regardless of how few times they are correct with their weather predictions. They base their forecasts on numerous support devices. Perhaps the weather can be more accurately predicted by other means. Maybe.

For example, my brother Philip is a farmer. My nephew Paul is a builder. They pay attention to the weather channel and news, but mostly their interest is the temperature and the weather radar. With that information, as well as looking at the sky at night and in the morning, they draw their own conclusions.

It is astonishing to watch television when a massive storm of any kind hits. The frenzied weather reporters are charged with enthusiasm. They are in hog heaven and the center of attention. Of course, everyone is tuned in to their television with each report.

This reminds me of a movie, *Good Morning, Vietnam* where the late Robin Williams was the main character. His radio broadcast monologue included a lot of chatter about the weather. One part of his dialogue was when he pretended to get a call inquiring of the weather. Robin's character said, "It's hot, damn hot! Open your door and step outside!" Maybe we should try that? Go outside and suck in a deep breath of the fresh air to see what it feels like. Then you can make an informed decision about your plan for the day. For good measure always take a coat with you. It is better to have it and not need it, than to need it and not have it. The same goes for the other things one carries with them in their car.

Anyway—our plan was to vacation in Florida for three sunny weeks in January. Lucky us. We left early Saturday morning the 12th of January when we were getting dumped with our first snow in central Indiana. We dressed like it was winter upon our departure. Two hours later when we landed in at the Clearwater airport, it was a balmy seventy sunny degrees, and I started stripping. Of course, we can't believe the weather forecasters in Florida either.

When I was a youngster, we loved big snows and storms in the winter. Of course, we wanted inclement weather to be so bad that school was canceled. My fourteen-year-old granddaughter thinks that way today. Some things never change. So school is called off, what happens then? Well, the streets are too treacherous to drive for higher learning, but not for meeting with friends to go sledding, to the mall, to the movies, or just hanging out. Does that make any sense? However, I know that is what we did as children also.

One thing for sure, we aren't shoveling our weather in the sunny south. Now that another massive storm has blasted our home in Indiana, we think, "We are vacation geniuses," for choosing to go south in January rather than wait until February as usual.

Eva, Georgiann, and Marilyn with me taking the selfie

I caught a beautiful wave in action.

On Facebook, there are many photos of the snow, empty grocery store shelves and apparently there is lots of French toast being made. All the bread, milk, and eggs are depleted. We sure don't miss home with the frigid snowy weather. A few days here in the sunny south, we've had to wear our jackets and sweaters. This is the Sunshine State, and the sun shines every day. Our mantra is, "Every lousy day in Florida in January beats a cold snowy day in Indiana."

Regardless, we count it all joy and a blessing to be on the sunny beaches in January. Each day as we walk on the beach, I am sure to take a selfie to send back home. I feel certain the recipients are exceedingly happy to see our smiling faces reflecting the sunshine and water. Retirement is great! By the way, I no longer live on Turkeyneck Hill, but my brother and his family does.

Me, Marilyn, and Georgiann on Redington Beach

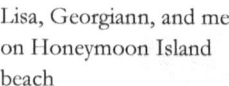

Lisa, Georgiann, and me on Honeymoon Island beach

I know I am not being kind, but the struggles of life have not always been easy for me. But thank God for now, I am in Florida attempting to become svelte, blonde, and bronze. Pray for me because I have become a "Vacation Genius!"

PS Could someone please go shovel my driveway while I am in Florida?

A piece of driftwood on Honeymoon Island beach

Exercising Can Be Fun

Lazy Rivers

Many people live a charming life whether they realize it or not. Unfortunately, some have a bad case of "FOMO." You've heard it before, the "fear of missing out." However, humans need proper maintenance from time to time. We wear out from age, abuse, neglect, overeating and laziness. We get tired easily, and it could be from lack of exercise.

If I had a dollar every time I heard someone say, "When I reach age 65 and get on Medicare, I am going to have ___ fixed," I'd be a wealthy woman. Astonishingly, Medicare insurance is one of the best things they created for the elderly. (I say elderly with chagrin, as age 65 seems like a youngster these days.) The next best thing is the Part D drug plans. The drug plans first appeared in 2006. Before that, each senior had to buy their own drugs, and it was a struggle for some people. Therefore, we need to remember the blessings which comes from aging.

In our youth we endured many scrapes, bumps, and bruises. We lived so cavalier and didn't worry about a thing. As the decades pile up, so do the conditions that slow us down. Even as young parents, we thought we knew it all. Boy, thinking back, we sure would have done a few things differently while raising our families.

In recent years, resorts, big water parks and even city pools have begun installing relaxing pools called, 'lazy rivers.' For those who don't know, that is a winding narrow swimming pool meandering in a loop. The water is about chest high. (I know, it depends on how tall you are.) They provide flotation devices like inner tubes. For the older set, many park departments open their swimming pool *lazy river* section every weekday morning at 9:00–but without the floaties. The seniors *walk with the flow.* Apparently eight circuits at our lazy river equals a mile, but no one knows for sure. Energetic walkers go against the flow   of the water. That's more difficult than it looks, bless their hearts.

It is amazing how buoyant our bodies are when we have a few extra pounds. In fact, I could walk backward, lift my feet up, and float down the lazy river if I wanted. No paddling. But I need the action of walking to exercise my body. Even my knees and hips appreciate the no-load workout. Realistically, this is a fantastic way to get full-body workout without load bearing joints feeling the burden. Plus, we enjoy fresh air and get a suntan to boost our outward appearance. Often a nap in the afternoon after a good lazy river workout is required. Most people walk for at least for two hours per visit. In that length of time, a lot of the world's problems are solved while making the circuits. Try it if you get the chance.

The Lazy River with Judy, Patty, and Georgiann

People might be too inhibited to go to the pool, but don't be. Everyone has the scars of life, and the purpose is to exercise. We are our own worst critic. The beauty is, we meet new and old friends and family to walk and talk with. The time flies while walking and we catch up on all the latest happenings in our lives in a couple of hours. At 11:00, the pool opens for everyone. That is when all the tubes get released into the lazy river along with swarms of children. Some seniors continue to float in the river, but most get out of the way of the energetic youngsters. I get out at that time; it gets too crowded with the tubes and the rowdy children.

Besides our bodies, everything needs maintenance. We need dependable transportation to get to the pool, work, school, and run errands. With that comes the responsibility of upkeep. First, the car needs gas to run. Unless your car is electric, then you need to plug in at night. Long ago when we first had automobiles, my Grandpa Charlie Dow wondered, "Would it hurt to run the car without any gasoline?" Of course, he was joking.

We all know autos must have regular oil and other fluids checked and changed. However, are we faithful to do it? One thing I know, if there is black smoke rolling out of your tail pipe, you might have a problem. After a long drive or a night drive in the country, a lot of bugs commit suicide on the front of my car and windshield. An application of Windex or Fabuloso works wonders to get rid of the bugs.

On the farm, our machinery often broke down in need of maintenance. I remember how often we used the grease gun by attaching it to the fittings on the equipment. I enjoyed pumping the gun until grease came squirting out the other side. Unfortunately, improper use of any equipment can cause malfunction and failure. If you are like me, the last thing I usually do in most situations—is read the owner's manual. However, at last resort, I read the owner's manual.

Whether we are talking about our bodies or anything else—we need to exercise careful maintenance. As many people say, "It's hard to get my biscuits and gravy to come out even." We have an expiration date and so does everything else. I for one wish to live as fully as possible my whole life long, and I know most people do too.

If you choose to try the lazy river, you will not be disappointed. Of course, walking, or other forms of exercise will work. Doing something is better than nothing when you decide to keep trim and fit. Just keep moving as much as you can. Unfortunately, we all know when we stop voluntarily choosing to move, it won't be long until we are not able to move. I love the lazy river.

Foodies, Their Foods, and Exercise

Folks, it's time to stop the madness. Have you noticed the grocery shelves? They started being empty during 2020. Every trip to the grocery, I have noticed shelves which are empty. It isn't always the same food groups or household and paper products. It's everything. Yet not all at the same time.

True, more people eat at home. With that being said, the portions are somewhat larger when serving favorite foods. The restaurant industries are suffering and all the people who depend on restaurants. Maybe they could get a job at the grocery stores. They are always terribly busy. Period.

If I were an entrepreneur, I'd start a business which teaches the basics of cooking. There are people who do not know the basics in food preparation. Classes for cooking and sewing was a prerequisite when I went to school. I don't believe it is any longer. Too bad. Not all parents and grandparents are passing down these skills. Truth be told, not all parents know the basics either.

Most cooking and preparation is easy, it's the cleanup that gets in the way. Who wants to wash the dishes along with the pots and pans? Not me. I usually keep them washed as I go. It makes the cleanup a lot easier when finished.

A large amount of the groceries being purchased nowadays are ready-made meals. The ones that go from the microwave to the table. That makes it easy. But fresh foods made from scratch may be better nutritionally, value, and more affordable.

The basics I would teach is how to make simple dishes that always comfort the whole family. It is good to know how to bake, broil, boil, grill, and sauté. Of course, knowing how and when to do these processes comes with practice.

Another thing to learn is when to use butter, oil, bacon grease, spray oil. After years of cooking, baking, and grilling, most of the simple tasks are performed with these, and without thought. Now if you want to bake bread, make homemade pie crust, or homemade pasta, that is not basic. Get a friend or relative to help you with those recipes.

Now that so many are preparing more food at home, it is possible the scales will continue to increase. Do you know someone who is losing weight? Anyone? No? Me neither. Everyone at my house has not lost any weight, but now the holidays are upon us. Now what we are going to do about that. I have a solution, don't get on the scales.

We all know of many fad diets and have tried them all. They all work period. When we go on our diet, we usually get off it. When that happens, our body goes back to the previous weight, if we are lucky. Often, we have added a few extra pounds.

Some people have a remarkably high metabolic rate who do not have a large appetite. Nor do they have a hankering for sweets. Those people usually announce, "All one needs to do is merely cut back on their eating and they will lose weight." Bless their hearts. High metabolism could be a genetic trait passed on from our parents.

A few nationalities have a propensity toward thinness, and we are so happy for them. My thought is, "I need to have a few extra pounds in case I get really sick, and it causes me to lose my appetite, then I won't starve to death." "Like I always say, it's a sorry life if you don't have something or someone to blame for the shape you're in." Of course, blame never helped anyone get healthy.

How about the *rubber band diet*? That is where you put a thick rubber band on your wrist like a bracelet. Then you mentally make a list of everything you wish to avoid. When you think about giving in, just pull the rubber band out and let it smack your wrist. Do that a few times and you will quit thinking about poor consumption choices. So far, I've broken several rubber bands and still could lose a few pounds. Try it and let me know how it works for you.

What is the answer? Eat things that agree with your body and mood. If it bloats you or gives you indigestion of any sort, don't eat it. That's it. Only eat when you are hungry, but who does that? Stay healthy. Moderation is the key to any consumption. "Consumption," wasn't that an illness back in the old days Yes! Tuberculosis (TB) was referred to as *consumption* or the *Great White Plague* for how pale their faces became when afflicted. In 1904, Dr. Edward Livingston Trudeau started what became the American lung. Association. At that time, TB was the number one cause of death in America. It took almost fifty years to eradicate the disease.

Anyway, regardless of your diet and exercise choice, always keep moving. Move in some form for about thirty minutes per day. That isn't much. After all, the last exercise we will ever do is walk. I encourage you to stay in motion by going for a walk. You will feel much better at any age.

Go Ask Alice — Bocce Ball

Have you ever played bocce ball? It's a peculiar game like bowling, shuffleboard, or the Olympic sport of curling. Bocce is pronounced, "bah-chee." Get it right or the old farts will let you know. Immigrants brought this Italian sport here; it's one of the oldest sports in the world. The word bocce in Latin means boss.

To start with, you have four players per team. Two players on each end of a long rectangular court measuring thirteen feet by ninety-one feet. The surface can be grass, sand, crushed stone, or in our case where we played in Palm Harbor, Florida is outdoor carpet over concrete. Each team has either four red or four green balls weighing two pounds each and are 4.2 inches in diameter. I suppose the red and green come from the Italian colors. The game also has a little white ball called a pallino, 1.57 inches in diameter and weighing a third of a pound.

After a coin toss to see which team goes first, the first player rolls the white pallino, which is the target ball, and one of their red or green balls. Then the other team tries to get closer to the pallino. That continues until both teams have rolled all four balls. The ones who have the closest ball or balls win the point(s) from that round. Then the other end rolls. The game we played in Palm Harbor was 14, winning by one point.

Someone has thrown the little white ball, and one of their balls

Having only played a few times so far, it isn't as easy as it looks. However, watching the people line up and throw tells me it is a patient and slow game. This game is well suited for this time of their lives and not for youngsters, but it is for all who are young at heart. I watch competitors with canes, and walkers stumble to the court and throw incredibly good balls. There were players who had their oxygen tanks on the sidelines to breathe from in between their turn. Some have been playing for thirty years or more and some, like me, have just started.

Like any game, there are a lot of rules and strategies to follow. The kind yet older population is sure to tell you if you

are doing anything you shouldn't. All the time. My team captain is Alice. The other players kept correcting me and finally said to me, "Go ask Alice." All I could think of was the song, "White Rabbit" by Jefferson Airplane, and when I got to the other end,

Another player throwing her ball.

I had a big smile on my face. Alice is a sturdy and sure octogenarian who doesn't take guff from anyone, including me. She is also a quick-witted and a dry-humored person. I believe she has lived a colorful life. So, I said to her, "They told me to 'go ask Alice,' —do you know that song?" She said, "Yeah, what about it." And so began a great friendship of like minds.

We also began playing euchre with Alice every Wednesday afternoon. Being from the Midwest, we know how to play, and it is fun to play even with those just learning. If you and your partner win, you move to another table and switch partners. It goes like that for two hours. No big deal, no teams, and no record keeping. Just playing for the fun of it. And guess what, Alice is from Indiana and plays euchre too. What a very adept card player she is. It is always a pleasure playing at the same table as her because Alice is a hoot to be around.

The older I get, the more I realize we only grow in age and little in mental maturity. (Unless we keep schooling ourselves in various intellects.) One thing I know, I've become more mellow with many ideas and issues. It could be I want peace of mind more than anything. Or maybe I just don't care. For example, playing pickleball in Florida is almost a full-time job. Same for golfing. I have found that I want to win, and I want the best score possible. But "Girls just wanna have fun!" Pickleball is played every night and most Saturday afternoons. If the ball is close to the line, (but probably out,) in the heat of the game-- it is in. Just play nice. I win enough and having fun is more important than anything. I love the social aspects of this sport. I have made many new friends while playing pickleball here and everywhere I have played.

Golfing is a pleasure I have enjoyed since the early nineties. Although, when I started playing pickleball in 2015, I decided not to play much golf, and I did not. However, here in Palm Harbor, the three nine-hole executive courses are included in the HOA fees we pay monthly, so we play golf too. The challenge is still present for golfing, at least for the short game.

Now, if I could only get Alice to play golf with me.

Tattoos and the Olympians

Do you love the Olympics? My TV used to be on from morning to night with the Olympics airing whether I was watching it or not. Not so much as I age. However, if you are like me, I'm impressed with all the sports and marvel at the competitive edge. These athletes are simply amazing. They have worked diligently at their craft to the point of perfection.

When I was a kid and in my early decades, no one had tattoos except Popeye and other sailors. Of course, motorcycle gangs and bad guys had them. Other than that, everyone is clean-- no ink. What happened? Are tattoos a rite of passage or coming of age, or what? Even the Olympians have put on body art/ink. The more dangerous the sport, it seems, the more tattoos cover their body. I'm not talking about just Americans either, most every country display tattoos.

Unknowingly, the art of tattoos has been around since the Stone Age. Archaeological digs have uncovered mummies with evidence of skin alterations in Europe. Tattoos began in the countries of East Asia, the Polynesian countries, and Russia. They were discovered by archaeologist in Greenland, Alaska, Egypt, Siberia, and South American countries as well. Evidently, this is nothing new. Tattooing was a way of tradition in many cultures and apparently used for identification. Some of those traditions still exist. Occasionally it showed ownership or that a person belonged to a certain region. North American Indigenous people highlighted their opinions of the world, as well as connection to family, society, and tribe by tattooing.

After the American Revolutionary War, sailors tattooed themselves to avoid British capture. Of course, the sailor had "Seaman Protection Papers," unfortunately, those papers didn't mean a thing to the British Sea Captains. They tore them to shreds or burned them. Consequently, it was common for sailors to garner tattoos which identified them as an American.

I remember when my brother George went away to the navy. When he came home on leave for the first time, suddenly there were tattoos on his forearms and upper arms. Actually, he got one the summer between his junior and senior year in high school while in Florida. This one was a heart with an arrow piercing through it. It read, "Dixie." The other two from his early days in the navy were in script writing, "Born to Lose," and "Born to Raise   Hell." I was flabbergasted at the sight. My brother had turned into a pirate, yikes. I was only ten and was not used to tattoos on the people I love. Those tattoos sure put a mark on him, or at least I thought they did.

During the Civil War, many soldiers who died on the battlefield, were buried where they fell. The families often didn't know where or when they died. Many of the surviving soldiers observed this and started leaving identifications on their belt buckles or sewed personal information into their clothing. Some made small metal disks with personal identification and wore them pinned to their clothes.

It wasn't until 1906 that the government issued *dog tags* for all service members. At first they included not only their name and branch of service but their next of kin and their address. The dog tags for the service members grew from then on. For those of you who do not know what a dog tag is, it is a lightweight aluminum silver identification tag they wore around their neck and never ever took it off while they were in the service. That practice is still used in our current military.

Regardless of the identity issue of the new beginning of tattoos, it has evolved. It went from the elite persons of society to the repulsive. Now more than ever, body art and modifications have become a new culture. People are more accepting of them in every facet of life.

The sophisticated have kept them off their visible skin when dressing for work. The professional athletes have gone a little crazy with the ink. Most people in Hollywood are using 'tats' as self-expression. Some everyday people who have tattoos place them in discrete locations of their body. Most aren't seen unless they go swimming.

Speaking of swimming, it's interesting to see older men and women at the pool or beach. Or when they wear shorts, and the old tats are revealed-- including on their lower legs or ankles. Better still, funny how a tattoo of Tweety Bird on the chest of a twenty-year-old, many decades later turns into a stretched yellow bird as gravity took over.

Rest assured; body artists are simply amazing. I stare at some beautiful work when I see it and often ask the tattooee the story of their ink. They are not shy and usually share their story with ease. The only thing, tattoos are next to impossible to remove. Like in the movie, "We're the Millers," the kid got a tattoo on his chest. It was supposed to read, "No Regrets." Instead, it read, "No Regrats."

If you are thinking about getting a tattoo, be certain of the *forever* expression on your skin. A friend of mine said, "If I ever get a tattoo, I will get a set of red lips on my right hip." Knowing her, I doubt that will ever happen.

One thing we all agree about the Olympics, tattoos or not, it sure makes us proud to be an American. Anytime there's an Olympic awards ceremony and the Star-Spangled Banner plays with the US flag rising behind the podium, I salute our beloved country, and I know you do too!

God bless America, even the Americans with tattoos.

Better Homes and Gardens

When we had the 2020 pandemic, we not only had a fantastic spring and great start to our summer, but we all had plenty of time to do the yard work. With so many people working from home or just sheltering-in because of that coronavirus, chores have gotten accomplished. It is unusual how many beautiful yards and gardens there were in the spring and summer of 2020.

During the first few weeks of the shutdown, we could only shop for essentials. It is surprising what was deemed essential. However, we are not the policy makers. We leave that to our brilliant and illustrious government leaders. Consequently, we were permitted to go to hardware stores, garden shops, or grocers. Basically, visit any store who sold food, drugs, or home care merchandise. Of course, the liquor stores were essential and remained open. I hear many drank more at home than normal. Some had new drinks they'd never tried before. Have you heard the joke, "Twenty years from now we will be governed by kids who were taught at home by their non-teacher parents who started drinking at 9 a.m.?" God help us.

Nationwide, statistics have shown the building supply and gardening industry had record breaking sales in 2020. Their problem was keeping merchandise stocked. It is no wonder everyone's yard and home is beautiful with all the attention and pampering during the spring.

Additionally, do you know that list of home projects and "honey-do's" we all make? They either were completed, or they simply grew into a full-blown remodel. Either way, most of us have cleaned out our houses, garages, and sheds. In the beginning, we couldn't give items at the donation centers. Now we can. I've noticed plenty of garage sales lately. Folks are ridding themselves of once valued treasures.

My yard is prettier than it has ever been. I have flowers in the front, side and back. When it doesn't rain, I sprinkle it with the garden hose. It's possible some neighbors might think that I moved and someone with a green thumb moved in. My working days have been over for several years and my yard could have looked this lovely all along. This year I merely got a bug from a friend to flower up. Everyone else was planting and making improvements, so I joined the cause. Ah, the pride of ownership.

My yard in full bloom

Happily, those pesky geese and ducks who like to fertilize and sleep in my backyard have been thwarted. My neighbor and I built a fence. It is not a big fence, but it keeps them on the lake side of the yard. This seems like a rite of passage. I now have dominion over my home and yard again. Hmm, when did I lose it? Now to keep this train rolling down the track.

Many *do it yourself* energizers have gained momentum. They keep looking for areas of the home and yard to improve. It is incredible what people can do if they try. With the growing number of people using YouTube for tutorials, the sky is the limit of doing hard tasks for yourself from now on.

The plus side of the epidemic is fascinating. Positive thinkers have taken on a new mindset and started looking at

life differently. Relationships have been mended, letters have been written, and many calls have been made. Families are coming together like never before. Some have become acquainted with each other again. Often under their own roof. Maybe this was part of God's plan. Shall we gather at the river—the beautiful river?

My beautiful lilies

The scripture of Ecclesiastes 3:1–2 "There is a time for everything, and a season for every activity under the heavens: a time to be born and a time to die," There are twenty-eight *"times"* written in verses 1-8. I believe the days and *times* of those scriptures have come to fruition before our eyes. Such as Ecclesiastes 3:2b "a time to plant and a time to uproot," and 5b "a time to embrace and a time to refrain from embracing." Then in 6b "a time to keep and a time to throw away."

Continuing in Ecclesiastes 3:12–13; "I know that there is nothing better for people than to be happy and do good while they live. That each of them may eat and drink and find satisfaction in all their toil— this is the gift of God." We indulge in tasty foods at last when toil at home. Hopefully, you have found this positive satisfaction as your gift.

Now let's remember the doxology, "Praise God from whom all blessings flow." We have much to be thankful for, especially with our better homes and gardens. Like a diet, it's not how much you lose, it's how much you keep off and remain fit. With confidence, your home will surely look picture perfect for months and years to come.

The Olympic Athlete

The 2024 Olympics are in the record books. If you were like me, you were glued to the television regardless of the hour. We saw the games live and then watched the repeats. There's something fascinating about the Olympics, especially when the Star-Spangled Banner is played.

The relentless dedication the athletes demonstrate is very impressive. At times, the wins and scores are closer than a gnats eyelash, separating first to last by mere fractions. Well, except for American Katie Ledecky in the 1500-meter freestyle swim, who won the gold by ten seconds.

It is humbling to witness less fortunate countries who can only send a few members to compete in the games. When they finish well, their country's joy explodes, and they embrace enthusiastic celebration. However, that is true for all nations when they win. Don't we love the competitive spirit of the athletes? Yes, we do.

I don't know about you, but it lifts my spirits to watch the games. Their athletic bodies are fine-tuned, even years and decades after they have retired from competition. For us non-Olympians, just exercising an hour per day would make an enormous difference in our physique, but we don't. At my age, I am content to walk a couple thousands steps per day. Of course, many of us are slowing down in our physical activity because of achy and stiff bodies. Maybe if we walked more and didn't sit so much, it would hurt less, but why take a chance? Right?

When I was a young girl, and even a young adult, I was quite active in various sports. When competing, I genuinely enjoyed the effort required. Now I play pickleball and of course, table games, and cards. Unfortunately, the table games and cards do not require very many steps unless I am getting up for snacks and drinks.

Recently, I accompanied my friend Georgiann and her two grandsons, ages seven and nine, to the Indianapolis Children's Museum. *What was I thinking?*

Georgiann and her two grandsons at the Indianapolis Children's Museum

After we finished four floors of the main museum, we wandered over to the *Sports Legends Experience*-- an extended part of the museum. There was a wide variety of sports to test our skills. Many enthusiastic kids, young and old, were trying their hand at the different sports. Basketball was one of them.

As a teenager, I was adept at the game of basketball. Of course, that was only a few decades ago. While her grand boys were trying their best with the basketball experience, I thought, "I can do this." Unfortunately, my muscle memory has *bitten the dust*. As much as I tried, I couldn't get the doggone ball up to the rim much less through the hoop. Finally, I succumbed to a two-handed, under-hand shot. The ball danced around on the rim but still didn't fall in the basket. After three under-handed tries, I turned around and there stood Georgiann. *Where did she come from?* She said, "I thought you were some kind of a superstar at this sport or was that just another windy tale?" My embarrassing response, "Look, smarty pants, that was only a couple million years ago. How long have you been standing there?" "Long enough," she smirked.

Unfortunately, when we stop an activity, the skill *can* stop too. Think of all the possible Olympians in the world who could have made the games if only they had the opportunity and time required to hone their craft. Many parents could not afford for their child to pursue the sport. We all know it takes a village and a lot of money to become a world class champion, much less finish the best of the best in the Olympics. Can you imagine ever winning a medal? One must dream big to achieve greatness.

In August of 2024 I accompanied a friend to a family wedding in Chicago. Although I didn't know any of these people, I accepted the invitation. To my surprise, the bride, was invited to the Olympic trials as a pole vaulter. Unfortunately, an injury and subsequent knee surgery thwarted her progress. However, she is in the Hall of Fame for her high school and college at University of Oregan. Along the way, her roommates and teammates at Oregon made Olympic teams. And guess what, three of them were at the wedding. I met three Olympians in one day after never meeting one in my life!

The one male I met has multiple medals, including gold as a record breaker in the decathlon from three different games. A Canadian lady has medals from two Olympics. The Belgian born phenom just finished competing in the Paris Olympics as a triathlete. This was her third Olympic competition. In Paris, she was unfortunate to swim in the River Seine which was full of contamination. No one had been allowed to swim in the river for over 100 years and now it was okay for open water swims. As a result, she became deathly ill and had to be hospitalized in Paris. This forced her out of the games. These three world class athletes blended in with the wedding guests until someone pointed them out. I sought them, congratulated them, and took photos with them. Wow, I was among greatness.

The bottom line, wherever you excel, pursue your gifts vigorously. Practice until you have them conquered. The Olympic athletes absolutely love their sport and do not wish to do anything else. The desire comes easy, the demanding labor is worth making an Olympic team. We all know of many athletes who were close to making an Olympic team, but something kept them from crossing the finish line. It's tough.

We need to *count it all joy* and a privilege to live in a country with countless opportunities of all types, Olympic or otherwise. Nonetheless, bless all athletes who have ever competed on any team. They don't need to win a medal; it's accomplishment enough just to make any team.

There's a Place for Us

Seniors and Smartphones

Isn't it a hoot to hear the various love-and-hate conversations from seniors regarding their mobile phones? Some love them and others detest them completely, along with those who use them.

Not too many years ago, I remember the old crank phone that hung on the wall in our farmhouse. I recall the mouthpiece we spoke into and the part we held to our ear. We'd give the crank a whirl to access the operator. It seemed we always had a party line with nosey neighbors listening in on our conversations.

Our current *smart phones* can be a friend or foe, depending on our attitude toward progress and change. I sternly resisted switching from my flip phone years ago. I'm finding it is futile to resist change, for change happens whether we like it or not.

Many years ago, I was in Martinsville assisting an eighty-three-year-old insurance client. I needed to speak with her carrier; therefore, I asked to use her land line to dial an 800 number. She responded by handing me her iPhone, as it was her only phone. I didn't know what to do with it. I still had a flip phone, so the eighty-three-year-old showed me how to use it! She was proficient in calling, texting, and emailing with her iPhone. On her computer, she did Google searches, perused Facebook, and sends emails. I was impressed with her gift of technology, and I told her so. She said, "Don't be impressed. It is my only way of keeping up with my grandchildren and great-grandchildren. Before, if I called them, I rarely got an answer or a return call. The text messages are most always immediate responses. Plus, I can stay up with their activities on Facebook!" What an exceptional attitude toward change.

When she walked, she was bent over almost to a ninety degree, and her gray hair swayed back and forth as she moved across the room. I told my adult daughters the story and stated, "I am ready for an iPhone." They were happy I didn't wait until age eighty-three and was bent over.

An older neighbor Donna had a flip phone until her husbands' sisters were in town. Their smart phones had GPS maps. Her husband Merritt saw how convenient the features were for directions in the palm of their hand. Immediately, he took Donna to buy one so they would have GPS also. Later, I showed her some tricks and shortcuts to use. She is happy with her phone now, which proves you *can* teach an old dog new tricks.

Modern technology is great but sometimes hard for older people to grasp. Donna loves the texting feature — for ease of communicating with her family, grandchildren, and friends. A small group of women gather at my home for *movie night* every Monday. One week, Donna was anxious to show off her oldest grandchild Andrew's photos on your new smart phone. He left for college and sent her a text photo of himself in his dorm room. She is so proud of Andrew and spoke of how he was awarded the 'best hair' in his high school class of six-hundred graduates. Andrew plans to cut his hair, and in the photo, it was much shorter. Donna showed the photo to everyone she met all week long.

This Monday, she came displaying her 'group text.' She was ready to read the groups' comments to us out loud. Donna is hooked on texting, especially with her grandchildren. Her granddaughter in Minnesota, Emily, texted to ask how cousin Andrew was doing at college. Grandma happily forwarded the photo of him in his dorm. Emily zinged back her response, "That's not Andrew!" After a closer look, Donna realized the photo was not her grandson at all. Who was that young man who bears resemblance to her grandson Andrew? Before Donna could send anything, she received another text photo from Andrew posing for his first day of college classes. There he stood, tall with very long 'new bleached blonde' hair! The boy in the first photo was his roommate with long hair, but much shorter than Andrew's.

Oh, the things we accomplish with smart phones nowadays! And to think, we once had to wait at least until October or Thanksgiving for our children to come home once they left for college. Now, if we want, we can FaceTime them daily on the smart phone. What used to require the space of a small home for a computer, now fits in the palm of our hand. In addition, the power of that little smart phone is infinitely greater than those first computers. Yes, we've come a long way!

Thank you for the technological advances, baby boomers! You took us to the moon and back! Now how do I turn this dang thing off?

Device Addiction

We all want to be happy, don't we? Sure, and many do whatever it takes to reach a blissful level. Some people strive for the extreme state of happiness called euphoria. Yet how do we get there?

First, how does one know when they are happy? Most of the time, people are happy and don't realize how happy they are until they aren't happy any longer. That is sad. It is human nature to desire happiness and with it comes contentment. After all, our Forefathers said so. After all, we live in America where we have many choices. We have the *liberty of the pursuit* anyway. In fact, the preamble to the Declaration of Independence states:

> *"We hold these truths to be self-evident, that all men are created equal, that they are endowed by their Creator with certain unalienable Rights, that among these are Life, Liberty, and the pursuit of Happiness."*

Digging around a little, I came across some particular *happy* hormones. A few of these I know firsthand, and they are important for good health. Natural endorphins are excellent. They make us happy and reduce pain. Pure dopamine is a feel-good hormone. I feel it when I receive 152 likes on my Facebook post or hit a winner in pickleball. Natural self-made serotonin is good for reducing depression and provides peaceful sleep. Each hormone does something a little different in our brains that affect our feelings and disposition.

Some happy hormones are a lie, a vexation to our spirit. Be aware of those. Years ago, people had pen pals. They exchanged letters from far away and sometimes other countries. But did you really know them? Were they honest? We never knew the truth as most pen pals never met. It still feels good to get letters and cards in the U. S. mail. If you don't mind, keep those cards and letters coming.

We have many addictive behaviors. Many are from our devices. Years ago, we had answering machines. Then email started; faxes came, and soon car phones were the rage. We couldn't wait to get home or work to check voicemails, emails, and faxes. The car phone was installed in our cars and not carried in our pockets. Plus, the minutes were few when using the car phone. Remember those days of very short conversations on our mobile phones?

Now we have an overabundance of internet diversions, games, and interaction with people through all our devices. Some people we know very well, and some not at all. They can be acquaintances or friends of friends. In fact, scrolling through those apps can be addictive. Have you ever watched TIK TOK or the reels on Facebook or Instagram? That's the app where people make a short video. They range from tutorials of useful information, telling stories, recipes, demonstrating athletic skills, or simply dumb stuff. Truthfully, I watch them and go down a rabbit trail. Before I know it, I have spent over an hour looking at crazy displays of humanity.

Remember when young kids *never* had a phone? That was a long time ago. Now we see many groups of people anywhere, all ages, all looking down at their phones and not to each other. I've noticed in restaurants and bars where there are sports on the televisions, they aren't glancing at their phones but engaging with others while eating and watching the games.

One March, I was on the beach in Florida. Sitting a few yards away were four women who appeared to be in their 80s. They were all mesmerized by their phones. No conversation. I almost took a photo of them. Could that be me someday?

They were probably reading the Bible and having a study later.

When television was introduced into every home in America, people predicted it would cause the breakdown of the family. Now we have a television in every room, and everyone has a phone. If you have a phone-- you have a computer and the pathway for every device addiction is possible.

A special discipline is required to say no to the distractions which pull us away from others. Some say with apps like Facebook, Instagram, Twitter, and other internet lures, they have many friends. Really? If you needed serious help, how many of those so-called friends would be at your side? Helping a friend in need is a friend indeed. Do any of those types of friends fog a mirror for you. Yes? Probably not.

I believe it is important to breathe the same air with your friends. Spend time close and in the same room. Everyone leaves a legacy of some kind. What will yours be? Is it surrounded by face-to-face relationships? What are your activities and actions? Do you merely spend hours in solitude staring at a screen? I hope not, yet we all do it a fair amount of time in today's world.

Maybe you have noticed our devices are a waterfall of unfiltered news and information, worthy or not? Years ago, a Norman Rockwell painting depicted a crowd of people at a train station looking down and reading their newspaper. They read it while standing on the platform awaiting their train. Was that considered addiction too?

Guess what? The devices know your interests. Your phone, computer, iPad, Alexa, and Echo are all listening to you. All the time. Mention something enough, and you will start seeing ads for the item on your devices. My sister and I have done that on many occasions and have proved it to be true. For example, we said, "Toaster oven," over and over in different sentences and sure enough, we saw many ads for toaster ovens on our phones and computers. Easy peasy?

During times when we are stuck at home, many become more addicted to devices because of isolation. Device addiction can and does harm relationships. Please don't let your human contact be lost. Every one of us need human interaction and touch. Devices can't give be personal like a human.

Let's step up to the challenge-- I'll go first. There is a place on our mobile devices to see how much time we spend on the phone. It is found in the settings under *screen time*. It tracks each day how much time spent every app on your device. Check it out. If you are spending way too much time on silly stuff, maybe it is time to have lunch with a friend.

Yes, devices can be addictive. Our habits define us, and our happiness comes where we make it. Just remember it is hard to have a device hug you back when life gets tough.

Visiting the Shut-Ins

What's become of customarily visiting shut-ins? A shut-in is someone unable to get out of the house on their own and is usually disabled in one form or another. Is visiting them still practiced? We still do but not as much. On the farm, we call livestock who are penned up in barns or sheds *shut-ins* too, but not in this context.

Do you practice active visiting at all anymore? The drop by to visit? No, it is not as common as long ago. However, I always welcome people dropping in for a visit. Of course, my house might be a wreck but that's ok.

Life in the country was quite simple when we were kids. Especially during the summertime. If the family vehicle was in the driveway, it often meant they were home. Therefore, if they were home, and/or sitting on the porch, it was an open invitation to stop in for a visit. Of course, that was long ago. Now we usually call first and ask if we could drop by for a visit. Even given those circumstances, you'd better have a good reason to merely drop in uninvited. Some don't know how to entertain drop ins. When people are recovering from an illness or are older, often those people are lonely. Still, we make sure it is okay to visit in case it is a difficult day for them.

On the farm, if a friend or relative visited and it was near mealtime, it was assumed they would stay to eat with the family. We'd set another plate, as this was a customary practice. Nowadays it's a big deal to make sure there is enough food. That really puzzles me. We have more food in our cupboards, refrigerators, and freezers than ever before. What is the concern?

What is one of the first things we learned when we went to Sunday School as a small child? Sharing. Yes, we learned to share. So, throw another potato in the pot, add another glass of sweet tea, and don't forget to pass the bread. How difficult is that? You would be surprised how that would throw many people into a tizzy.

Recently, our cousin Wyatt took ill and was shut in. George, Lois, and I decided to visit him and his wife, Linda, in Gosport. We called ahead to make sure he was feeling up to visitors and the time was set.

Not long before this, our brother George went to the funeral of a classmate. He stayed afterward to patronize a new restaurant in Paragon. This new establishment happened to be the very spot where our dad's favorite tavern stood for over seventy years. Recently it was totally reconstructed and is a beautiful addition to our old stomping grounds. As it turned out, the owner's family was also born and raised on Turkey Neck Hill.

George insisted that we stop there for lunch on the way to our visit with Wyatt. In our family, we have nicknamed George. It's *Velcro*, a very fitting name. It does not matter where we are-- on a cruise, in a faraway state, around home, or our 'old stomping grounds'—George 'trees someone in conversation.' He causes us to wait until all the seemingly useful information is fully exchanged.

Sometimes that is a good thing because he uncovers some interesting facts. Mostly, it simply delays our progress. All things considered, we know this about *Jorge'* going in and we adjust our plans accordingly.

Now that I write columns for the newspaper, George is sure to ask the people of Morgan County, "Do you get the newspaper and see my sisters' stories about Life on Turkeyneck Hill?" I am so delighted he gets a kick out of those columns.

We heard there was a new bakery in Gosport, so we stopped there as well. While in Gosport, we toured around the small town where our mother was raised. We drove past our grandma's home where we visited often as children. It was pleasant, but everything seemed so small in size compared to our memory. We used to be very small too, so everything is in perspective according to our memories.

Our visit with Wyatt went quite well. We covered all the mutual relatives in conversation, and we spoke fondly of all our children and grands. He was much improved, and we were all so happy for our visit. Our promise was to do it again soon. I pray we keep that promise.

We enjoyed our lunch at the new restaurant in Paragon and even stopped by on the way back home for a cup of coffee. Of course, George was again scanning the restaurant to see if there was anyone to which he could talk. Luckily for me and Lois, he did not *attach* to anyone.

It appears the older we become, the more a good nap is necessary in the afternoon. Hence the coffee. It was wonderful to have lunch and then go for a visit. However, falling asleep while calling on a shut-in is still considered impolite in most circles.

I encourage you to visit your friends and family soon and often. You never know when the time will be too late. "The highway to heaven is paved with good intentions." (anonymous) As usual, bountiful blessings followed our family visit from that day.

Expensive Naps, Water, and Matches

One of the many blessings of growing older in our retirement years is taking naps. It becomes a part of our everyday routine. Of course, since we are no longer getting paid for service, we have daily chores which need to be completed. I think most of you will agree.

A habit of doing laundry and washing the sheets on Monday is a good one. That way I remember the last time I changed my bed. Sometimes in the warm weather, I still hang my sheets outside to dry. The refreshing aroma of the line-dried linens is almost intoxicating. Being raised without a clothes dryer back on the farm, we always hung laundry on the line outside or in the basement if it was too frigid for outdoors.

While in Florida for the winter, a few times we went to the movies on Tuesday when the cost was only $7.50. One movie we saw should have been a block buster starring Anthony Hopkins. It was titled *Freud's Last Session*. I was interested because it was based on true events. I like those kinds of stories, based on true events. Supposedly, Freud was counseling C. S. Lewis as World War II was bearing down on England in 1939. Freud was ill and died a few months later.

The flick was slow-moving and sometimes hard to understand their English dialect. All the moviegoers were in recliners (which most theaters have now). About a third of the way through the show, several were snoring. In fact, one man in the row behind us was extremely loud. It got to be quite entertaining when we thought of the ticket price, $7.50. So, we called it an expensive nap. If you saw the Anthony Hopkins movie, *Remains of the Day*, also starring Emma Thompson back in 1993, it was a snoozer too. There is no guarantee a star will always have a hit.

In February, I flew home from Florida for a week. While waiting at the gate to board, I bought a twenty-ounce bottle of water. It costs a whopping $3.42. I couldn't get the lid off and had to ask a young man to open it for me. (I must be getting frail.) Spending that much on a bottle of water caused me to wonder. I figured out how much a gallon would cost at that rate.

$$3.42 / 20 = .171 \text{ cents per ounce}$$
$$171 \times 128 \text{ ounces} = \$21.888 \text{ per gallon}$$

As I tapped my credit card to pay, the gal at the cash register asked, "Do you want to add a tip?" I didn't reply, but I wanted to say, "No, if I did, the tip would be, go to Kroger and buy a whole twenty-four count case of twelve-ounce bottles for $2.99." However, I kept the snarky comment to myself and just pressed the no tip button.

Consequently, while at the airport, I decided to people watch. That's how I entertained myself for the last twenty minutes until we boarded the aircraft. This made me ponder, should I be thankful for the price of gas? Does this help me put things into perspective? Well, not really.

Let's talk about a gallon of milk for a moment. It provides nourishment enough to sustain life. It also costs less than the twenty-ounce water bottle at the airport. Plus, milk provides nutrition, food, and fuel for the body. Sure, water can prevent dehydration but at what cost? It is the convenience factor that drives costs up, right? Plus being at the airport. Remember that old adage, location, location, location.

This is how weary retirees look at life. They observe things and form opinions. What else do they have to do? When they get the chance, some of them bore you into a coma talking about all their opinions. Or they write columns.

In the process, I was thinking about matches. I miss matches, do you? Remember the olden days when every restaurant, hotel, gas station, and other businesses had free matches? They left a box or a bowl of them sitting on the counter and were free for the taking. They are extremely useful, cheap for them, and provide advertising. They also doubled as a place to write a note if you didn't have any paper handy.

Do kids today even know what a match is? (Unless it's a dating app.) Nah, it's gone by the wayside along with crank phones, rotary dial phones, manual typewriters, and the yellow pages. Just to name a few.

Morale of the story: If you ever have trouble sleeping, just go to a boring movie, and forget purchasing cheap refreshments while there. Since most people do not smoke anymore, light their trash in the barrel out back, or light the fire in their furnace, you won't need or find any matches--unless you go to an estate sale.

The Home Search

How far does a friendship extend? Do we merely meet to share a meal? Do we visit and give care while hospitalized or while recovering at home? Do we take short or long vacations with them? More specifically, "Should I go house hunting with her in Knoxville?"

My friend Georgiann's (then) five- and three-year-old grandsons live in Knoxville, Tennessee. Moving is in her future as she can no longer resist not being in their lives on a daily or weekly basis. My daughter, Jessica, is a realtor in St. Petersburg, Florida. Georgiann called her for advice and asked her to refer a realtor in the Knoxville area. She found and referred Beverly, a reputable agent to help to take the scary out of her search. The time was set and soon we took a road trip to meet Beverly for a house hunting excursion. It has been a while since I have been privy to the rigors of house hunting. Fifteen years ago, I searched out the house I live in now and it seemed a lot different from the search we endured in Knoxville.

Oh my gosh, we visited twelve houses on Thursday and ten on Friday which proved more exhausting than I remember. Keep in mind, I am fifteen years older too. The whole experience causes me to ponder, "What was I thinking?"

On the first day while sitting at a stoplight I noticed a storage unit with a sign which read, "Volunteer Storage." Speaking without thinking I asked the realtor, "I see the Volunteer Storage sign across the street. Is that as opposed to forced or mandated storage?" Bev, the realtor, softly replied, "You might remember the state of Tennessee is the Volunteer State. Also, Knoxville is home to the University of Tennessee Volunteers. So, no, I don't think there is any forced or mandatory storage in Knoxville." Needless to say, that little flub of mine caused much comic relief throughout the remaining time spent in Knoxville.

The sign I saw that day

We lodged at a motel which provided *free* breakfast. (Of course, we all know the cost of breakfast is included in the room.) I purposely suggested staying at one offering a waffle maker with breakfast. I believe it is the little things in life that makes all the difference. For me, waffles for breakfast while traveling are one of those indulgences.

While eating the *free* breakfast we watched the TV news. Apparently, Tennessee is proposing to increase minimum wage from $7.50 per hour to $15. "Are you kidding me?" The ones reporting for the state argue that people can't provide for their families on minimum wage. Excuse me, but I thought, "Minimum wage was never intended to be the sole income for '"making a living,"' was it?" Again, what do I know? "Isn't the minimum wage designed for employers to have employees perform simple tasks which required very little training or intellect?"

A business owner reporting on TV stated, "If this law passes, I will be forced to let people go." I don't have a formal education nor training in economics besides the school of hard knocks. However, it seems to me if the cost of goods go up, the consumers cost will go up as well.

The subject matter brought people together in the breakfast room. A young blonde, blue-eyed fourth grade teacher from Kentucky spoke up. She said, "This is ridiculous to double the wage. Why not raise it a couple dollars to start? I teach in Kentucky and there hasn't been a teachers pay raise in over 20 years." My thought is, she could sell real estate on the side, but the process is rather arduous.

The time spent in Knoxville was a crash course in real estate education, what people should or shouldn't do to sell their homes, and how big the business of flipping houses has become. That house flipping business is for the younger generation because there is a lot of sweat equity involved.

These few days gave me a sincere appreciation for the real estate agent. They work for free unless a house is sold. We can retrieve just about everything online these days, so do your homework before you go out with a realtor. It's important to respect their time too. I told my daughter, "Zillow (a real estate website) reports the owner bought this house in 2016 for $220K." Jessi replied, "In real estate we say the "A" in Zillow stands for accuracy, ask Beverly for that information." Of course, the joke is there's no "A" in Zillow.

The bottom line, a little success was had on our mission to find the perfect house. Georgiann did make an offer plus she became really familiar with the area. The best part was she got to have dinner with her grandsons and put them to bed.

In the whole scheme of things, yes, friendship do stretch to going house hunting with them. Now Georgiann only needs the accepted offer and she's ready to move to her new home.

Do You Want Some Fries with That?

Fries. As in those delicious French fries. They are deep fried in fat with salty goodness. Enough salt to make your blood pressure rise in a few minutes. Yes, the advent of fast food was all the rage in the early years of my childhood.

The hamburger mega store began their business in California in 1955 and has spread all over the world now. What I like best about McDonald's is that it's a respite of familiar junk foods when traveling abroad. Not necessarily nutritional but familiar. We like familiar foods on long trips. McDonald's franchises became the benchmark for the franchise industry.

My first experience with a McDonald's restaurant was the one at the north edge of Bloomington, IN, on State Road 37. The early ones only had walk-up windows to place your order. A few years later, they enclosed the area for ordering so they could be open year-round.

The famous hamburgers were only fifteen cents each. Of course, this was in 1961. I remember they served Cokes in a paper cup with no ice. The Cokes were ten cents, one size. One thing that stuck out in my young mind the first time I visited McDonald's was the statement the staff asked after we ordered our hamburgers, "You want some fries with that?" That took me by surprise, and of course I did want some fries, especially theirs. But I didn't always have enough money to purchase a hamburger *and* fries.

I was with my sister Clara, her husband Frank Allen, and their four children the first time I saw the McDonald's restaurant in Bloomington. It had the golden arches with a sign sticking out that said, "15 Cents," and another statement below indicating how many hamburgers they had sold. I remember when that number was "1 million Hamburgers Sold." It was hard for my small mind to wrap around one million of anything back in 1961.

Clara and Frank had a station wagon for their family vehicle. I don't remember the brand, but the third-row seat faced the back. So, the kids saw where they had been but not where they were going. At the time, their four children were Debbie, age four; Patty, age three; Cheryl, age two; and Randy was just one year old. With no seat belt or car seat laws in place yet, the kids roamed all over the car as they drove down the road. Often, they fell asleep on the seats or the floor. That was typical for the day in the life of families with children. This was one of those days when I was twelve years old and tagged along.

As Frank stopped the car in front of the drive-in McDonald's restaurant, he asked me, "Sadie, (That was his nickname for me back then.) do you want to go with me to place the order and help carry the food and drink back to the car?" Clara and the four kids waited in the car. This was quite an experience for me. The all-new and shiny red and yellow eatery was bright and fascinating to see.

When Frank got to the window, he ordered, "I'll have ten hamburgers and six Cokes." At the time, they had milk shakes, orange drink, and Coke. Not diet Coke nor any other flavors. Of course, the server asked the question to Frank, "You want some fries with that?" He looked at me to see what I thought. My expression was one of big eyes and desire. Frank agreed, "Sure, we'll have three orders of fries." The Cokes and fries were ten cents each. So, ten hamburgers, six Cokes, and three fries equaled two dollars and forty cents. Back then, we didn't have sales tax.

We carried the fast food to the station wagon while all three of the kids in the back were eagerly hanging out the side window. Little Randy was on Clara's lap watching us from the front. As we ate the hamburgers and fries in the car sitting in the parking lot, it was love at first bite. And consequently, it was the beginning of trust in the American explosion of fast food. It still exists in every food variety to please every palate.

The old time McDonalds restaurant

In fact, some people become so hooked on fast food or the speed of it, they have lost control of their nutritional needs. But it sure tastes good going down, especially the fries. However, recently while traveling, we stopped at McDonald's. Our order was one a quarter pounder, one fish, one fries, and one medium drink. A whopping $14.15 for that small order. My how times have changed. One can only imagine what Frank's order would have been in today's money.

For me, I now prefer to eat at home even though I still go out for the social aspect of dining. Nevertheless, every time I hear that old question, "You want some fries with that?" I am reminded of a simpler time and place of my childhood.

Seniors Go for Good Eatin'

After retirement, many seniors have a habit of meeting friends and family out for breakfast, lunch, or dinner. Not all the same people on the same day but a lot of eating out. This is a friendly way to get out of the house, be sociable, and not make a mess in our own kitchen.

In fact, many retirees meet weekly on the same day, same time, and at the same place. Others meet monthly or every couple of weeks to eat, play cards, dominos, Maj Jong, or other games. Therefore, they have something on their calendar besides possible doctor appointments. When gathering, they often solve the world's problems and discuss the latest newsworthy topics. Plus, seniors share their latest illnesses or injuries; all while receiving quality advice from those who have had similar conditions. Comparisons help drive away fear. Hence, the advice is priceless and always correct, right? If you don't have a group who meets regularly, maybe you should start one of your own.

There are multitudes of interesting eating places to meet, eat, and gab. Some are out of the way places like in small towns within an hour of home. However, we can't go too far— we must be back to our easy chairs for our afternoon naps.

When we discover a good eating place, we tell others and go back with new people. A couple of years ago, my friend Marilyn took me to Morgantown for lunch at this little dive. It was worth the drive. They had a very large menu and even open-air seating for warm weather. You should try it out sometime. Just go to Morgantown, you will see the green building.

Southwest of Martinsville on State Road 67 is Paragon. This is near the farm where I was raised. Paragon has two locations to enjoy some good cooking. You probably know of many yummy eateries all over the map worth taking the drive for appetizing cuisines.

About two years ago, I was with a friend from Tennessee doing business in Seymour. I used to live in Scottsburg for ten years (about twenty minutes south of Seymour) and have many friends in those southern counties. Of course, I know a lot of good eatin' spots. I remembered this family café where they served the best homemade coconut cream pie. When we were finished with our business I expressed, "Let's go to the Townhouse Café for a sandwich and some pie. They have the best pies of all kinds, especially the coconut cream pie." It was almost two o'clock, and I knew the lunch crowd would be gone. When we pulled into the small parking lot, there was only one car left in the lot.

As we strolled toward the door, a worker walked out the back door and stated, "We are closed. We close at 2:00 most days unless we have cleaned up and we have no customers then we leave earlier." My friend said, "Darn, I heard you had good home cooking and the best coconut cream pie." With that she looked at my friend's car, saw the Tennessee license plate, and replied, "Did you come all the way from Tennessee?" "Yes, I did."

The staff member continued, "Well, hold on a minute, I will get you two pieces of pie." With that she went back in the café returning with a whole coconut pie in a box. "If you have come this far, you need the whole pie." I offered her twenty dollars, and she said, "No, we have already cleared the drawer, this one is on the house. You enjoy the pie, and the next time you are in town, come back before 2:00."

We were like two kids who accidentally got locked in a candy store with no one watching. However, we didn't have any forks. Consequently, we hurried back to Greenwood to eat a piece of this delicious coconut cream pie. It did not disappoint our taste buds, and we had more to share.

Last summer we were back in Seymour and set our hearts on eating lunch there, and, of course, having more pie.

Unfortunately, the little café had closed. What a huge disappointment. Apparently, the owners retired, and no one wanted to continue the restaurant.

Here is one last story about my friends who live in the sleepy town of Poland, Indiana. Their pizza joint is in the middle of town. Yes, Poland, population 97, is west of Cagles Mill Lake on State Road 42, southwest of Cloverdale. This crossroads town has a few businesses and a few homes. The people are friendly, and the pizza is superb. There is another restaurant and a couple of shops for the traveler who wanders into this little piece of heaven. For a beautiful and easy country drive, take a trip to Poland, Indiana. You will be glad you did.

Do seniors love the out-of-the way places and the small-town eateries? Yes, we do!

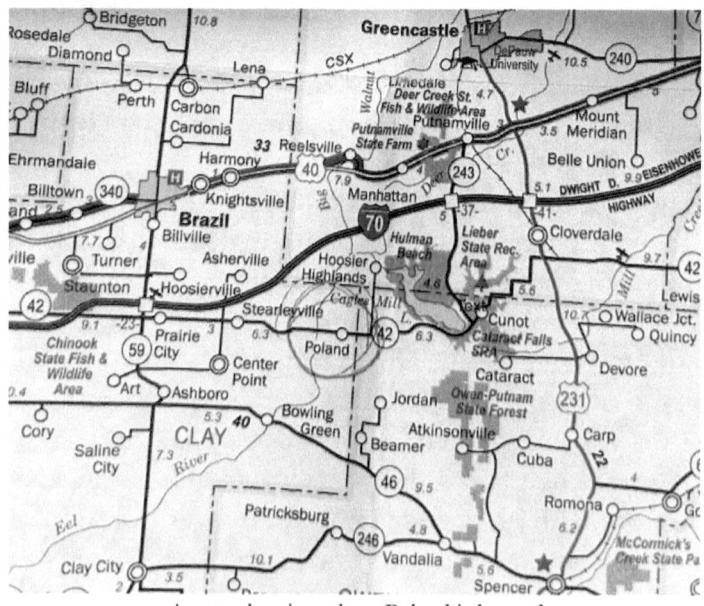

A map showing where Poland is located

Hey, I Wrote a Book!

Have you ever wanted to write a book? I thought about it for years but never did. Then in 2018, I was privileged to offer columns for the Martinsville, IN, newspaper on the opinion page. I was allowed to write anything that came to my mind. Many of the stories involved growing up on the family farm near Paragon with my two brothers and three sisters. Some columns were informative, and many were filled with natural humor. I enjoy writing these tales and when meeting with my siblings, they still tell new stories from those days of our childhood. Even though we all live in the city now (except for brother Philip), we relish those years.

However, many of you know that I wrote my first book, *Life on Turkeyneck Hill: A Memoir*. It shared many of those same newspaper columns. The book went live on Amazon, February 29, 2024 (Leap Day). The first day it sold forty copies. What? Two weeks later, I received fifty author copies. The book sold over eighty copies online in one month. By that time, the eBook was made available to the public, and a week later, the hardback was out.

I never knew all the "behind the scenes" processes which occur when books are published. Now I do. The next book will go smoother. Yes, I finished writing a second book. It took a while to get the manuscript to the publisher for editing and formatting. Of course, *More Tales from Turkeyneck Hill* is finished and was available as of July 17, 2024.

The first fifty author books I purchased of the first book were sold while I was still wintering in Florida in 2024. By the time I arrived in Tennessee on the way home from Florida, I received another 100 paperbacks and five hardback books. Many of them sold rather quickly in Tennessee. Therefore, another 100 were ordered. Recently, I ordered ten more hardbacks, and now I am waiting on my third 100 paperbacks. After all, one cannot go to a book signing without any books to sign, can they? In total, I have purchased many books to sell.

One might think that this is a money-making proposition but hold on to your hat. Many tenured authors advised me as a first-time author to price my book around $10. So, I did. Many known authors can fetch upward of $20-$40 for their novels, but I am not one of them—yet.

Book signing at the Whiteland Library with my daughter Katte

Nevertheless, I keep books in my car. I have a small backpack with five or six books beside me everywhere I go. Every day. When I play pickleball, go to restaurants, to the bank, to retail stores; any place I go, they are with me. One never knows when one will run into an old friend or acquaintance. They might ask, "What have you been up to?"

That just opens the door for me to do a *show and tell* of my book. Often, they buy one or more on the spot.

When I strike up conversations with servers, cashiers, or bank tellers, and so forth, I eventually say, "Hey, I wrote a book!" Or ask them, "Are you a reader? Of books?" They are all interested. Many are readers and want to buy it. Some grew up on farms or visited a farm as kids. Several have said, "I love to read memoirs but had never met the author before." I am delighted to sign their book. It has been a joy.

Our neighborhood recently had a community garage sale, and I sold several books to people I did not know. How nice. I'm finding that people are hungry for books to read. They like to read lighthearted, warm, and clean non-fiction books. That is what my books provide—authentic experiences, entertaining, inspiring, and happy ending stories. Some people bought additional copies to give as gifts. What a sweet and kind compliment. Thank you all.

Studies have been done regarding authors and writers. Of all the people who have ever wanted to draft a book, only about 4 percent of them have ever written their first book. Of that 4 percent, only 2 percent of those ever wrote a second book. It gives me pleasure to write, and hopefully readers enjoy my stories. Thank you if you are one of the people who have read my books. You are kind.

Without a doubt, this has been one of the most rewarding experiences I have ever undertaken or tried since giving birth to my three daughters, having a granddaughter, or at age fourteen giving my life to Christ. The most satisfying events of life are not about money, but relationships. I am showered with countless blessings from God. I trust and hope your life experience is as full as mine.

At the *Correspondant* newspaper office book signing with another happy customer.

Relating in Various Ways

Lucky to be Born

Are we lucky to be born? Is it chance or destiny that we are here? Did we exist because of God's divine providence or are we merely a random act?

When we think about the millions of possibilities or chance meetings by all our ancestors which were necessary to produce us, it boggles my mind. In reality, why think that hard? Who are we? What draws people together enough to cause a connection which turns into marriage, or at least a relationship which brings about new life? The odds of a new life are pretty slim if we think it through. So many people needed to come together and have children for us to be a descendant.

Let's talk about love for a moment. What attracts us the most about another person? I'd say a plethora of character traits. First and foremost is proximity and availability. If you are not with someone or they are otherwise unavailable, there is a fat chance you will meet for a future relationship.

Second, personality and like core values must match to a certain degree. It doesn't hurt if you are both from the same socioeconomic scale but even that is not a deal breaker. Without a doubt, social and financial conditions change. To have a lasting relationship, all these changes along with our emotional maturity must grow together.

My parents, Harry and Dortha, were on a double date which turned out to be the date of their lifetime. The couples switched partners, and my parents became love birds. Soon they were married. It was a wild and wonderful story of my parents—for twenty years. If that hadn't happened, I wouldn't be here. Numerically, I was their sixth "feather in his quiver," as Dad liked to call me. Dad didn't have any Indian roots, but he used that analogy just the same.

Harry and Dortha had a precise chemistry in their marriage that one could call their initial encounter—

providence. After all, it built and has continued a dynasty of sorts for the Dow legacy. To date, their union has a current offspring totaling over 106 living souls. That number includes the in-laws, steps, adoptions, as well as blood lineage.

Now each of their six children have their own lineage to build their personal legacy. My argument implies— the responsibility for keeping the family together lies with the elders of the family. As a parent, we are mother hens with our wings spread gathering our chicks into the fold. Otherwise, they scatter and become distracted easily away from the core family.

During the coronavirus quarantine of 2020, many have responded by doing things they have put off for years. Besides cleaning your homes and garages, some have contacted long lost relatives and friends to spread a little loving kindness. It's comforting when I get a call, text, or email from folks I haven't spoken to for a long time. That makes me feel special.

As the song lyrics says, "love is a many splendored thing." We all need and want to give and receive love. When we are young and in love, sometimes we are just in love with love, not the person of our affections. There should be a rule of some kind that keeps couples from moving too soon into the area of commitments. But those rules will never happen. I like a rule to be, wait four seasons of life to see if it is true.

Serendipitously, out of the blue, people often fall in love without ever planning to do so. They can't get the other person out of their mind no matter how hard they try. That, my friend, is the best kind of love. Few truly feel that love, and if they do, it is rare and normally doesn't last very long. Unfortunately, the fire dims. Of course, there is always the exception.

Yes— we are lucky to be born, and our days are numbered. I believe in Psalm 139:13,14 which says, "For you created my inmost being; you knit me together in my mother's womb. I praise you because I am fearfully and wonderfully made." Also, Jeremiah 29:11 "'For I know the plans I have for you,' declares the Lord, 'plans to prosper you and not to harm you, plans to give you hope and a future.'"

Faith is available to all. If you don't have faith, just grab ahold. We shouldn't live in fear; we should count our joy every day. Although it is sad for the ones who are directly affected by the illnesses like COVID, cancer, or many other disabilities, because of them, many are reaching out and touching family and friends like never before. Guess what? That is the way it should always be.

Then, 1 Corinthians 13:13 "And now these three remain: faith, hope and love. But the greatest of these is love."

I am content and privileged to live through such a time as these. It is the struggles of life which define us, mold us, and shape us into who we are or will become. In fact, it is times like these that we may shine and show the world our value to others. Whatever you do in life, promise yourself to have few regrets and realize the respect of life.

Out of the Mouth of Babes

If you spend a lot of time around youngsters, you will agree they say some amusing things. Coming from a large family, most of us are eager to strike up conversations with children.

In June, one year when Clara was first in the nursing home, a little four-year-old boy came to the garage sale we had for Clara's belongings. We figured he lived with adults because his level of communication skills was high. Debbie was painting the service door to the garage with white paint. He said, "Back in the day, I bet that door was blue." Debbie responded, "Why do you say that?" "Because if I had a door, I would paint it blue," he replied.

I was stationed by the money table, and I asked, "Hey little boy, what's your name?" He had a funny look on his face and told me, "I am not supposed to talk to strangers." I thought to myself, "He didn't have any trouble talking with Debbie." His grandma told him, "You can tell her your name." He promptly stated, "My name is John Wayne B., what's yours?" I said, "I am Phyllis, the ladies over there (pointing), are my sisters, Lois and Carol." He asked, "Who's painting the door?" "Oh, that is Debbie, my niece." Then John Wayne asked, "Do you all live here?" I said, "No."

He whined around wanting assorted items at the sale though his parents and grandma kept telling him "No." I politely invited him to pick something out of a *free* basket on my table. He was glad about that.

While his family shopped for over an hour, little John Wayne kept the conversation alive with all of us. Before leaving, he proudly announced, "I am having my fifth birthday party next month, and I want all of you to come! It is going to be at Aunt Mary's home because she has a big house. You must be careful because she has new carpet." He went on to say, "Bring me a present but don't tell me what it is. I want it to be a surprise. Be sure to wrap it but don't put it in a bag, I like to unwrap my presents." Lois asked him, "What kind of a present should we bring?" "I want any action figure, but don't say what it is out loud," he begged.

As the blonde-headed little fella was walking away from us as he left, he threw up his right hand and loudly said, "Later." I think he had watched adults make that gesture before. Grandma told us his birthday was November 30. What a handful he might be in years to come.

From 1996-2005, I lived and sold insurance in Scottsburg, IN. Often, one of the agents brought her elementary aged son Eric and daughter Laura to the office after school. They liked coming into my office because I always offered them the hard candy on my desk. I enjoyed their company; they were well-behaved, and I found them quite entertaining.

After a few months of Eric and Laura visiting me, Laura asked, "What do you do all day?" I told her I visit businesses to sell insurance to their employees. She said, "Seems like to me all you do is sit at your desk every day and talk on the phone." Bless her heart.

About ten years ago, a certain chicken franchise restaurant was labeled as a much healthier choice for children than the popular hamburger joints. When my great-niece Maddie and my granddaughter Maisy wanted to eat at that chicken place, they couldn't say the name correctly. Maddie called it "Chick Away" and Maisy, "Chick Fur Lay." They are age twenty now, yet the adults still refer to it as "Chick Away and Chick Fur Lay."

Currently, those two girls think that the coffee house from Seattle, which charges six dollars for coffee, is the cool place. I don't know about that.

The early 1970s was the advent of zip codes when people actually used them. One Sunday night at church, they spoke of the importance for young children to know their personal information. Things like address, zip code, phone number, and parents' names. The first part of the Sunday night service, the children joined all attendees in the sanctuary with their parents for the opening. During this opening is when the *information* discussion took place. I leaned over to my four-year-old daughter Kitte and whispered to her, "Do you know our zip code?" Kitte had the hymnal in her lap flipping the pages as if she were looking for a song. She replied, "Yes, I know how the zip goes, I know how to button, tie, and snap!" I decided to wait for a better time to school my three girls on such things.

Of course, we all have numerous stories of children we could spend hours telling and retelling. What a joy to reminisce, especially when we recall what the children in our lives have said.

Cloth Diapers and Rubber Pants

Can you remember ever wearing a diaper or soiling yourself as a child? I don't. I'm sure most of you don't remember either. However, these days during a hardy laugh, tears sometimes run down my legs, but that is not what we are talking about.

Back in 1972 when my twin girls were only twenty-six months old, I went to the hospital to give birth to my third daughter. This was the first time I was ever separated from the twins, and it was for five days. That was a long time for me and for them.

Before I was full term, the girls had been potty trained for several months. They were cute in their little white cotton underwear too, I might add. Due to separation anxiety, the girls reverted to wetting themselves or not quite making it to the bathroom. While I was still in the hospital, their dad decided he would not put diapers on them. It seemed diapering was not his forte. He claimed because he was lefthanded, he could not manipulate the diaper pins appropriately and therefore could never get the diapers tight enough to stay up on his toddlers. I never figured out why left handedness would be a cause. His recourse was to simply use a white cotton panty. For safety's sake, he added rubber pants *just in case.* We all know that was a recipe for disaster.

Grandma Betty (his mother) flew into Pittsburgh, PA, from Martinsville, IN, to rescue him and the girls before and after I came home from the hospital. This was back in the day when people could go clear to the gate to welcome them from the plane. His mother described her son approaching the gate after she disembarked. "There he came— a rambunctious child under each arm. I noticed him gripping white soggy panties enclosed in rubber pants in each hand." Betty continued, "The kids were so excited to see me they didn't notice or care they had bare bottoms." Grandma took the girls to the bathroom to clean them up for the ride home.

It wasn't long until the girls continued using the potty whenever they needed to go. However, for a few weeks, I had three girls in diapers. These diapers were cloth diapers. Do you know what they look like? The ones that sagged when full. The diapers that gave a good diaper rash if it wasn't changed soon after it was filled. They were extremely uncomfortable. Therefore, it was truly a big deal to potty train the young ones as soon as possible for them and their mother. Someone once said, "If they can walk— they can go to the bathroom on their own."

When I was in the first grade at Paragon Elementary in Mrs. Wershing's music class, I was incredibly shy. (I know, no one can believe that I was ever shy.) Unless the whole class was excused to go to the bathroom, I just held it. Well, I had to go bad and thought I would just let a tiny little bit escape. We all know what happens when we do that— yes? You guessed it, a flood came out all over my skirt, down my legs, in my socks, and dripped behind the metal chair onto the floor. Who knows what the kids behind me thought? I never turned around.

After all the kids had left the room, I remained in my chair. Mrs. Wershing asked me, "Phyllis, why aren't you going back to your class?" I started crying and replied, "I peed my pants." Then she readily saw the problem. That little stunt never happened again.

My friend Niki taught physical education in an elementary school. Each new year Niki said, "I don't look forward to the little first graders and their wet socks." Me: "Why are their socks wet?" Niki: "Guess."

Today's diapers can stay on a child through the night and not cause a problem. No rash, no chaffing, no problem. They can remain on them all day with the same results. Then comes the pull-ups. They stay diapered in them for an extended amount of time with no ill effects. We have six-year-olds in kindergarten and first grade still going number two in their pants and not thinking a thing of it. Sometimes they even go in their big boy or big girl pants. What has happened to training?

I can safely say that neither I nor anyone my age can ever remember getting our diaper changed. Some of us might remember wetting ourselves because we waited too long, but not in diapers.

Cloth diapers were effective and inexpensive, but they weren't comfortable. It was also plenty of work for our moms to wash those diapers. With my girls using cloth diapers, I washed diapers every day. That was motivation enough for me to train our girls to be responsible for the waste removal portion of their hygiene.

These days, what's the hurry? Is potty-training just one more thing for parents to do in child rearing? In a world of so many more modern conveniences, we can sometimes overlook basic disciplines for children.

Well guess what? It isn't the grandparents' job, so pass me another pull-up!

My Three Daughters

There is value in being the last of six siblings. I was fortunate to have many nieces and nephews during my youth, and I babysat many of them while we were growing up. Finally, I met and married a man named Bex. It wasn't many years before we were expecting our first child, or so we thought. As it turned out, our first was twins. What a double joy for us, especially me. The education gleaned from watching my nieces and nephews really came in handy. I also read Dr. Spock's book about child raising. What a crock of nonsense.

Two years later, we had our third daughter. Mothering is a love of the deepest form I never knew was possible. These three wonderful daughters have delighted my heart with a depth they do not understand. But other parents know what I am talking about. I have cherished their very existence since birth. My love for them knows no depth and will remain with me all the days of my life.

Kitte, Maisy, Katte, Jessica, and me on a cruise ship in the inside passage of Alaska

Although my three daughters never have said anything, I think they wonder why they have yet to be the subject of one of my stories. The stories have centered around me and my siblings growing up on the hill, and other crazy things that cross my path.

Recently, my three amazing daughters and I went to Nashville, TN, for a "Bex" girls weekend. Along for the ride were my (then) fourteen-year-old granddaughter and her girlfriend. We get away occasionally to draw closer in a world that seems to tear families apart. During our trips, I usually have discussion topics should the air ever grow silent. Silence rarely occurs, as each daughter is eager to tell their stories. As I watch and listen to my daughters interact, I behave like a kid in a toy store. Life just doesn't get any better for this mama.

In Nashville, we were privileged to visit John and Martina McBride's recording studio, called Blackbird Recording Studio. My friend Eva's son Brian works at Blackbird, so he gave us the grand tour. Keith Urban was recording there the day before. Darius Rucker, of Hootie and the Blowfish, was in one of the ten studios recording before we left. We all found the studios interesting, including my granddaughter.

Twelfth Street in the Berry Hill area is a happening place, so that is where we grabbed some lunch. While there, we visited "Draper James," a boutique owned by Reese Witherspoon. While touring Nashville on a Gray Line bus, we saw many highlights and heard the history of earlier years.

The Ryman Auditorium surprised us with its beauty, acoustics, and size for the time period of its original construction. By the end of the day, we had walked all three floors of the huge Country Music Hall of Fame and Museum. The beautiful downtown has grown exponentially in the last twenty years. A must see.

From the top of the Ryman
Auditorium

L to R Maisy, Jessica, friend,
Kitte, Mom, Katte in front

While the others were at Starbucks, I ventured to a grill
for a Coke. Unbeknownst to me, they came behind me waiting
on a bench. While I was at the counter paying for my drink,
my granddaughter Maisy was saying, "Hey, isn't that *THE*
Phyllis Bex, the one who writes columns in a newspaper, the
one who is from Turkeyneck Hill? Hey, Phyllis Bex, is that
really you?" I didn't hear a thing. Finally, I heard my daughter
Katte laughing as I turned around to leave. How sweet of
Maisy to make a funny like that about me. I loved it.

Arriving back at the condo, Kitte laid down while the rest
were eating snacks, kids braiding hair, and otherwise
enjoying conversation. I had received an Amazon Echo for
Christmas and did not know how to use it. Maisy's friend
Carly set it up, and we played with it. I even set the alarm for
the next morning. When we were playing Phase 10, I tried to
ask "Alexa" a question. "Turned that thing off," Jessica said.
"She was eavesdropping with her blue lights going around."

156

The next morning, after packing the cars, we drove to the Gaylord and the convention center. What a beautiful garden and conservatory. We were all enthralled at the enormity and number of Kodak moments. Our day ended at the Opry Mills Mall before heading home. A perfect weekend.

All my girls live very productive and busy lives. I marvel at each one as they display a servants heart in their own way. It does my heart good to know how much they love God and serve in the name of Jesus. Katte sells insurance, living near me in Greenwood. Kitte sells insurance in Charleston, South Carolina, and Jessica sells real estate and is living in St. Petersburg, Florida.

At last, my three daughters' wishes would be fulfilled. Truth be told, they are scattered throughout many stories. Blessings are all mine.

Angels Unaware

Like many people, angels have visited me. Often, they are unrecognizable, but they are angels just the same. Hopefully, you will be reminded of possible angel appearances in your life as your read the following accounts.

In the 1970s, a friend of mine attended the Benedictine College in Atchison, Kansas. Once she went home to Saint Louis, then took the bus when she returned the next week. Friends from Benedictine promised to fetch her from the bus station in Kansas City, Kansas, an hour from Atchison. Upon arrival, she heard her name over the PA system. The friends left a message saying they couldn't come for her. She had no money nor credit card (like most college kids back then), therefore, she was stuck. In desperation, she begged compassion from a taxi driver for a free ride from the Greyhound to the Trailways stations. The bus fare from Kansas City to Atchison was a mere $2.40. Suddenly, a blonde, blue-eyed, slender college-aged student laid the $2.40 on the counter for her fare. On the bus, *Michael*, the name he went by, told his stories of college life, easing her anxious mind. Benedictine is a small campus with great familiarity. After arrival, he disappeared, and no one knew of this young man. Amazing, he was an angel unaware.

In the early 1990s, I sold insurance near Terre Haute, Indiana. It was a rainy day. Heading to my appointment in the country, I stopped in Brazil, Indiana for gas near the I-70 exit. Pulling up to the pump next to me was a hearty, middle-aged man in a loud, old Lincoln— an "Uncle Buck" car. He said, "Woo wee! Is it raining or what?" I smiled and replied, "Yes, it is." I asked, "Are you from the area, and if so, do you know anything about Logan Creek Road." He said, "Yes, don't go there." He warned, "The road is flooded, and it will only worsen as the day progresses." I thought to myself, *well, darn, I don't get to try to make a sale, but yay, I am not going to get stuck in a flood.*

I went inside to use the bathroom and to pay for my gas. Then I confirmed with the clerk, "I hear the Logan Creek Road is flooded, do you know anything about that?" The clerk asked me, "Who told you that?" I said, "The man out there in that heap of a car." He said, "Ma'am, you are the only customer I have had the last twenty minutes." I replied as I looked toward the pumps pointing and said, "There." The car was gone. The clerk called a friend who lived on Logan Creek Road to verify the information. Sure enough, there was a flash flood over the impassable road. The Uncle Buck gentleman was another angel unaware.

Except for the intake nurse Debreia, my follow-up visit with the cardiologist seemed routine. She is a sturdy forty-something, six-foot-tall, ex-high school basketball player and not someone to mess with. I was fearful when she called my name, and usually I am not afraid of anything or anyone. Her long hair was filled with dozens of braids. In fact, her long braids covered her name tag. Debreia said her father must have fallen into the *vowel pool* when he named her.

During the intake, I discovered she is the mother of five children, including triplets, but birthed only her eighteen-year-old daughter. "Where did you get the other four?" I inquired. As it turned out, Debreia had been a foster mother for eleven years. The twelve-year-old had been with her for three years, and the ten-year-old triplets for five months. I asked her, "What are their stories?" "I don't ask questions," she said. "My job is to love these children in the trenches of life—to show them how to live with respect and to know they aren't judged nor mistreated. I merely love them just the way I receive them." I thought to myself, "Wow, what a testimony."

Before bed, she instructs them to brush their teeth, and they do. "How do you do that?" "First, if they don't brush their teeth, I tell them the tooth fairy will come and pull all their teeth," she responded. "Second, if they don't go to sleep, the Sandman will come with buckets of sand to throw in their eyes." She sounded intimidating to me and if I were a kid, I'd do whatever she asked.

Observing her stature and hearing her booming voice, I believe anything she tells me. However, it was the love beaming through her eyes that told a true and beautiful story. Disney or cartoons *are only* what is allowed on television; she doesn't want them to view questionable programs. Debreia's foremost concern is nutrition, hygiene, and no *nappy* hair. Therefore, haircuts are in order monthly. She pursues outside activities and sports as a healthy part of child rearing. The love she shows to them, by her voice, and reflection of them is immense. Bless her, as she truly is an angel unaware.

Maybe you have had similar experiences and have never realized they were angels skirting around your existence. Thank God for the ways he provides and protects us in our everyday lives. One thing to keep in mind is the following scripture from Hebrews 13:2

"Do not forget to show hospitality to strangers, for by so doing some people have shown hospitality to angels without knowing it."

Monday Night Movies

For several years, I have hosted movie night on Mondays. The same four gals mosey over for a night of mutual entertainment and laughter. It all started back when the series, "Downton Abbey" was released on DVD. Movie night never ended when the series did.

At the time, the group consisted of two preachers' wives (PW) who keep us on our toes and out of "R" ratings. Currently, one gal is eighty-one, another seventy-seven and the remaining three are young seventies. This bunch shares plenty of history and enlightenment. We listen intently to one another's challenges and triumphs. It is quite a learning experience to hear the stories we all share. The older and wiser PWs have personally served in ministries most of their lives. However, some of the stories they spill each week are rich and ripe in their own way.

We begin each Monday evening in collective amusement while gathering around snacks in my kitchen. In fact, our shared woes and fun stories trigger giggling which often make our sides and faces hurt. Even tears dribble down our legs at times. The personal stories are often prefaced by saying, "What is said at movie night— stays at movie night." They forget that I'm always in search of good fodder to use in my stories. However, I chose wisely as a show of respect.

Marilyn, Daphna, Donna, Georgiann in my kitchen.

While I was filling our glasses with ice, one PW reported, "You can't give me too much ice. I love ice but I don't crunch it." My reply was, "Really, why not?" She informed us in her authoritative voice, "They say the practice of chomping ice is a sign of sexual frustration." The other PW, who is an RN, said, "I heard it causes constipation." "It could be both," I added, "but as we age, I think our teeth become brittle and are susceptible to breaking." Who knows? Our comments aren't fact-checked for authenticity.

As the conversation ensued, one mentioned an old gospel song. Those two old PWs were struggling to remember the lyrics as they mouthed the tune to "Let's talk about Jesus." While they struggled along, I retrieved the song on my iPhone and turned it up. There was a video of the Oak Ridge Boys singing it with the Bill Gaither band. One recognized the piano player and told this story:

"Long ago, The Gaither Vocal Band was on an Alaskan cruise. The piano player, Anthony Burger 44, had a heart attack and died." How horrible. "What did they do with his body," I asked? We figured they had three options. Put his body in the cooler until they reached shore, fly him home at the next port, or bury him at sea. As it turns out, the Gaither's were not on an

Alaskan cruise but in the Caribbean when poor Anthony passed away while playing. ("I'll Fly Away" maybe?)

I remember a cruise joined by my sister Clara; we went to the Bahamas back in 1987. The first morning we arose to walk on the outdoor track as the sun was rising. We noticed at the rear of the ship a few crew members were doing something peculiar. *They were performing a burial at sea.* We witnessed the ceremony from high above. It scared us to watch yet made us wonder who was missing. From then on we kept counting heads, making sure it wasn't any of our people.

The PWs began talking about laughing in church and how inappropriate it can be. We have all been there. That's when the least little thing causes uncontrollable snickering, yet we cannot laugh out loud. Everyone has been in situations with others where no sort of laughter   is appropriate and because of that, everything is funny. We have friends who we would never want to sit next to during serious times because they make us laugh at everything.

The PW continued, "Back in the late 1970s, a small

mission church in Bargersville had revival meetings. Many came forward and twenty converts needed to be baptized. Since there was no baptismal at their little church, they borrowed the church where we ministered, Calvary Baptist. The time was set for two o'clock on Sunday afternoon." She recants the story, "As my husband and I arrived back at our church parking lot, there was the revival preacher in

A little Jesus. "Everyone needs a little Jesus! Right?"

his little car with one of the converts. This preacher was small in stature being about 5'4" and weighing about 140 pounds. The convert with him was 6'6"and over 300 pounds. I wondered how this baptism was going to work.

"As the little preacher began to baptize him, he pronounced the statement of faith as usual. Toward the end as he was beginning to dip the big fella, he hurriedly finished with a flurry of words. The big guy went down in the water and so did the little preacher. I was so tickled by the event I had to leave the sanctuary."

These stories which pour out each Monday night are endless, and I hope our moments together on Monday nights remain endless as well. There will come a time when we gather and sing "Will the circle be unbroken?" But for now, we cherish our Mondays together. However, it has turned into a daytime card game because no one wants to drive in the dark, and most of us fall asleep on the movie. *The love we share as we tarry there* is almost like heaven. We have grown close over the years and will remain close until the last one remains standing.

Natural Disasters and War

The time has come when we look back on the COVID-19 storm of 2020 and have vivid memories of where we were and what we were doing. Before it was over we all knew someone who was seriously affected by the dreaded coronavirus. Some have lost loved ones. Enduring this reckless calamity became something to be respected and feared. Hopefully, all of us found a silver lining.

Not long ago, one of the worse disasters in central Indiana was the flood on 6/7/8 or June 7, 2008. That day was definitely, "a Red-Letter Day." Most remember the flood and how it affected them. It took many families a long time to recover from their losses. The flood hit neighboring communities and was hard to fully comprehend. The ripple effect left a mark. That is the way it is with all natural disasters.

My niece Loida was married in Indianapolis on June 7, 2008. Sadly, many family members from Morgan County were flooded in and could not attend. The retention pond behind my home in Greenwood, Indiana, had risen well into my yard by the time I arrived home from the wedding. In fact, the water was licking at my back doorstep. Another foot higher and it would be inside my back door. There was nothing I could do but watch. The rain finally stopped and so did the rising waters. My neighbors and I were spared.

Other extended family members were not so fortunate. They lived along State Road 37 in Martinsville. That area flooded because the Jordan River couldn't hold back the deluge of water bursting out of the clouds and down the hillsides. Water filled their homes and basements to the point of them riding in a rowboat to escape the flood. It was a flash flood.

Powerful hurricanes blast the coastal regions. Usually, they have strong warnings. The evacuation routes guide residents to safety. I wonder if the hurricanes will subside this season because we have enough other disasters to deal with.

Springtime tornados sweep across the land leaving behind a path of destruction. We are warned to take cover. Most do and are safe, but the recovery is overwhelming just the same. Once we heard the locomotive sound of the tornado when we were on the farm. I remember standing at the front door watching the wind swirling the tops of the tall pine trees in our front yard. The tops were trimmed off as the tornado flew overhead but luckily didn't swoop down on us. I realized later how dangerous it was for me not to take cover, but instead to watch the tornado.

Forest fire disasters burn acres of land out west every year destroying homes, farms, and communities. Along with the dryness comes sandstorms in the deserts. We don't know much about sandstorms here in the Midwest. I can only imagine what that must be like.

The coronavirus of 2020 and beyond was and is a silent and sneaky enemy who has come to destroy us. Unlike anything our age has known before, it affects the globe. Has anyone personally witnessed such a tragedy? Probably not. Our memory of this event will take on a new dimension. A dimension like, "Before coronavirus and after coronavirus." How did we spend our time during the most adverse days? It defined our character. Some of you choose to follow the rules of quarantine and some did not. Those that did not were sure to share with others unknown. That generous gift continues when people's agenda is more important than the greater good of the masses. Like taking a flight or going to large events, if you feel unwell and it could possibly be the flu or COVID, the polite action would be to shelter in place.

On a lighter note, I heard a radio segment asking people to phone in telling how they handled the quarantine back in 2020. The stories were as expected then came the fun responses. Like, "On the first day of quarantine, my wife, kids, and I ate all the snacks. The next day we went to the grocery. Then the third day we ate all the snacks again." A lady called in to say, "When I was a freshman in college, many gained weight calling it, 'The freshman fifteen.' The way we have been eating, we could gain weight and call it, 'The COVID 19.'" Another gal called, "If you aren't a baker, stop buying all the flour!" Evidently there was a shortage of flour.

The last time we had a global epidemic of this magnitude was the Spanish Flu of 1918. I knew nothing of this occurrence until COVID-19 broke the news. Apparently, World War One came to an end resulting in a quick and high death rate. The 1918 flu was over-shadowed by war numbers. However, many people have grandparents who died in that Spanish Flu epidemic of 1918.

Here's the biggest difference in all of this. We can see, touch, and feel the presence of natural disasters or wars. The hardest part with a coronavirus is a battle against a ghost each day for prevention. Hygiene and social distancing is an effective deterrent, but even then, that sneaky virus bug crawls through the cracks.

As Christians we must always remember the promises of God. Here is one of many from Joel 2:25-26,

> *"I will repay you for the years the locusts have eaten—the great locust and the young locust, ... You will have plenty to eat, until you are full, and you will praise the name of the LORD your God, ... "*

When struggles are among us, most of us are willing to do whatever it takes to get our lives back to a new normal. I hope and pray God blesses you and your loved ones. Above all, I hope you find multiple silver linings where you can for any adversity and all the disasters of your life. Confidently, living on the promises of God is always a good thing.

A Friendship Letter

The following is a letter I wrote to my dear friend Daphna, when she was given a surprise birthday party on her eightieth birthday. Her daughters made a book of the letters which people wrote to her. This letter is mine.

Where do we begin? We all begin a friendship somewhere, don't we? Back in 1989, I was prospecting to find new businesses who would allow me to sell Aflac to their employees. We met when she worked for Corinthian Management up on Eighty-sixth Street in Indianapolis. As it turned out, she allowed me to go into six different nursing homes if their nursing home administrators would allow it. They did and the rest is history. Daphna even sold Aflac for a brief period and did very well. Then she got back into the nursing home business until now.

Daphna and I have remained good friends ever since that moment in time. We may be quite different in some ways, but one thing is sure, we are transparent with each other to the core. I make her laugh, and she makes me laugh. Isn't that what good friends do?

Anyway, we have often traveled together. The trip to Florida in 2016 was a riot. I asked her to put her things in two small bags, small enough for her to carry up to the second floor of my condo. It was a two-story walk-up. When I went to her home to pick her up, she came out to my car with this very large bag, a smaller bag, and a large purse. She stood at the trunk and looked at me. I guess she thought I was going to lug that huge thing in the back of the car. I gently said, "Grab a hold of one end and help me get it into the car." She did. Daphna politely announced, "I don't have two small bags, and I need my stuff." Of course she did. She can be so special.

Upon arrival to my condo in Clearwater, I let her know that I was not toting that big suitcase up the stairs, she would have to figure it out on her own. I have a bad back, poor knees, and know my limitations. So, I went on up to take a load, and as I started back down the two long flights of stairs, I heard a thump, thump, thump! It was Daphna rolling her suitcase upstairs one step at a time. By the time she got to the top of the stairs, there were several people outside their condos looking to see what all the racket was about. Pretty funny.

We had a wonderful week on our Florida visit. On our way back home, she wanted to stop at an antique mall close to the Florida/Georgia line off Interstate 75. We did, and she found her set of China displayed and purchased six cups and saucers. She only needed two, but they sold them by a set of six. We traveled on up the road.

A couple of hours later, we stopped at Chic-Fil-A for lunch, but we kept driving while eating in the car. We put the trash in the bag and moved it to the back floorboard. Later at the next gas and potty stop, while Daphna was in the bathroom, I opened the back door to remove the trash and put it in the trash can by the pumps. We stopped for the night somewhere around Dalton, Georgia. The next morning, I took my things out to the car and saw the Chic-Fil-A trash bag. That was strange, I threw away the trash bag from the day before. I thought maybe we had more trash. No harm, no foul.

Not long after I dropped her off at her home in Greenwood and I was at my home, I received a call from Daphna, "Phyllis, do you have my teacups?" "No, I don't have your teacups, you took everything that wasn't mine." She insisted, "Please go out to the car and look for my teacups that I bought at the antique mall." My car was empty by this time, but I looked anyway. They were not there. Sure enough, I threw her teacups away at the gas station, when I thought I was throwing away trash. The teacups were wrapped in newspaper in a white plastic bag. I tried to pay her for her teacups, but she wouldn't have it. "Daphna, I still owe you for those teacups, truly I am sorry I threw yours away. Sorry."

When I accompanied her to see her niece Brandi in Oklahoma City, Oklahoma, that was another fine ride. While trying to navigate the busy streets of Oklahoma City, Daphna had her OnStar, and I had my Google Maps from my iPhone. They were both talking but not exactly taking the same route. Finally, she told me to, "Turn that thing off or I am going to throw your phone out the window!" I promptly shut it off. We laughed hard about it later.

While at the hospital, we saw Brandi in her injured state and prayed over her. She was on the fourth floor and Daphna doesn't do elevators. I told her, "I am not taking the stairs down. Especially since I had not had my knee surgery yet. Four flights were three too many." So, reluctantly, Daphna got on the elevator with me. As our fortune would have it, they were doing construction on that end of this huge hospital. So, the elevators were padded and looked scary. Also, as the doors were about to close, two mean-looking construction workers boarded the elevator with us. Daphna looked at me with that deer in the headlights look. I knew she was not only afraid of the elevator not opening, but she also did not wish to be stuck on the elevator with those workers. She had nothing against anyone, she was just unsure and lacked confidence that we would go down and the doors would indeed open at the bottom floor. The doors opened just fine, and we got out of there unscathed. In her fear, she informed me in no uncertain tone, "I will never get on an elevator with you again." I told her, "Fine, but the grace of God was with us and here we are!" I love to tell this story on you, Daphna; you survived an elevator ride!

Anyway, Daphna, now that you are old enough to retire at eighty, you are old enough to ride an elevator and pack light from now on. After all, you are on a fixed income! I love you to the moon and back! May God richly bless you now and forevermore as he has all your life. You are one of my best friends. I have known about this surprise since the end of January. Can I keep it a secret? Yes I can!

We began as friends through selling insurance and thank God for Aflac that we did because we have a rich history of friendship and love! Happy Birthday!

Proverbs 11:25 *A generous person will prosper; whoever refreshes others will be refreshed.*

Retail Therapy and Black Friday

Shopping has never been my cup of tea. Even shopping online makes me queasy. Sometimes it's a job that cannot be ignored.

For example, to host a homemade Thanksgiving dinner, one must go to the grocery. I tend to procrastinate doing the things I don't like. I have ordered online from the Kroger grocery store for a curbside retrieval. I made a list on Friday, but didn't get to Kroger until Tuesday night. Unfortunately, I had to brave the focused group of shoppers in every isle. It was a mad house.

Clothes shopping for myself is the dread of all evils, yet we do need to dress ourselves. I buy a couple of the latest items a few times a year, and I am comfortable with that.

On a recent trip to Europe, I met a salesclerk from Chico's. I love that store, but it's pricey to me. True shoppers know when to shop the sales, but that's not my forte. She and her husband were on the same tour for eighteen days. Ms. Chico saw my wardrobe, and I think she assumed I needed new clothes. Or perhaps, she wanted to make a sale.

Ms. Chico invited me to her store, so I went. She kept bringing more items to the dressing room saying things like, "Do you like this?" "Oh, look at this, doesn't it look yummy?" I told her, "Yummy is a Long's donut, not clothes!"

Actually, I rather enjoyed my personal shopper. The clothes looked amazing on, and I felt good about myself. After trying on clothes for over two hours, I was tired, and my forehead was moist. That was work. A handsome sum was paid for the twenty-two classic items, but I was satisfied with my selections. However, given my approach to spending, I won't need to repeat that for four or five years, right? At least the day was full of laughter while shopping.

Black Friday is a totally different animal. I'm guessing people come *into money* at Thanksgiving. Charging is easy for

Christmas gifts or for themselves. The draw is the *big* sales. True, many are big sales. Some people save money for this day. Once an item becomes yours, it often loses its value. At times, it is cast away or jammed in the back of a closet. Who knows what happens to the gifts we give. But give anyway, it's the thought that counts. Those credit card bills come every month. The tingly thrill of purchasing becomes a heavy and dreaded burden for some when the bills arrive. True, the joy of retail therapy shopping can have its downsides. Be sure to choose wisely.

My friends Dolly and Marilyn wanted to go to the Edinburgh Outlet mall on Black Friday. I said, "Okay," because to me, it would be less crowded than the malls. Boy was I wrong. Those outer-lying parking spots that looked wasteful all year long, were full. Plus, they parked in the grass. We finally found a parking spot and went to the shoe stores. It seems these woman don't have enough shoes. Dolly bought seven pair of Clarks and then said, "Can we take them to the car?" "In a moment," as I was in the Bass store, still shopping. She waited with Marilyn who was already having issues standing. A bench in the warm sun called to them while they waited for me. When I met them, Dolly asked, "Could you get the car, we don't want to walk, and you can't carry all the bags?" Keep in mind, there are no parking spots. *Do these two old heifers think I'm their servant?* I made a mental note, *Shop with younger friends.*

I drove the car to them while fighting traffic and people. While they were getting in the car, they both said, "We're hungry, let's go to Montana Mikes." Creeping traffic stalled a quick exit to the restaurant. After we ate, we moseyed back to the stores. Ah! We saw why traffic was sluggish, a cop was directing the bottlenecks. Maybe traffic control is the first job out of the academy? Seems no training is required, and therefore, nothing is expected.

Shopping was dandy, even with the mass of people and lines. Unmoving while waiting to exit the parking lot, Dolly confessed. "When I used the restroom, I didn't notice I was in the men's restroom until I saw the men's sign on the door, and the women's was across the hall!" Her admitting she went to the men's room was stellar. Marilyn and I sure didn't see that coming.

We found bargains, bought many gifts, and had a memorable day! If you go shopping, you may as well make it fun. Enjoy your days of seasonal and therapy shopping!

Everyone...Meet Maisy Rose!

Don't we all believe we have the smartest, prettiest, kindest, strongest, and most wonderful grandchildren? Isn't that what we all say and want? It is amazing what love does to us in the form of a grandchild. You know, the child or children you get to spoil and then send home? This kind of love comes in a grand form. And I love it.

My daughter had been married for over eleven years before she conceived, and at three months, she miscarried. Losing the pregnancy was tough for the whole family. It was like a death in the family for all of us. However, one night, God made a promise to me that I would have a grandchild, and His promise was worth waiting for. In fact, we lived in the hope, believing it would come true someday.

After a year of healing, Katte was expecting again. Her new pregnancy had many challenges and health concerns. However, Katte's motherly instincts were steadfast. It was as if her positive attitude and willful spirit enabled her to make it to full term. She prayed. Thank God he answered her prayers. Of course, there was a whole army of prayer warriors praying for her and the pregnancy.

The modern hospitals are amazing with the layout of the birthing room. They are different from thirty-two years ago when I last delivered my daughter. I had not been present for a delivery where the labor room, delivery room, and staying room were the same room. They have a place for the father to sleep now as well. I understand how those arrangements are everywhere. However, they were new to me.

It was a cold and snowy day in November 2004 when the time came for Katte to give birth. Starting at 7:00 a.m., David, her husband, rushed her to the hospital. We didn't know what to expect with this being Katte's first full-term pregnancy and delivery. Katte has two sisters, and this baby was the first grandchild in our immediate family. The excitement and thrill of a new baby was overwhelming for all of us, and our emotions ran high. We just could not wait to hold that newborn baby.

As the hours flew by, it was certain this baby was not going to be an easy delivery. Katte was miserable after twenty hours of constant labor. Apparently, though the baby initiated this birth process, both mother's and child's lives were in jeopardy. The baby's elevated heart rate was constant for far too long. Katte's blood pressure was skyrocketing, and danger was lurking with every passing moment. The doctor decided it was best to perform a cesarean section. This would create an increased likelihood that both lives would be saved. I was for that option.

My first concern was my daughter's safety, which was my imminent and my innermost prayer. At 4:20 a.m., the team was ready for the surgery procedure and down the hall she went. Of course, my son-in-law David was with her the entire day, never leaving her side even in the surgery room. Hearing her bed being wheeled down the long corridor and facing the knife sent chills of fear deep into my soul. Trust was the only thought I had during my prayers, and I held on to that trust with everything I could muster.

What seemed like an eternity was less than an hour to bring forth a new branch on our family tree. Katte and David decided early in their expectancy not to have the sex of the baby revealed to them or anyone else in the family. Furthermore, they never revealed their chosen names for either a boy or a girl. This baby was going to be a true surprise for everyone. Just like in the old days.

At last, we heard the news that the mother and baby were healthy and normal. Hallelujah! As those of us remaining at the hospital waited, we moved to the hallway outside the room she was originally assigned. We felt we could have a better vantage point to see Katte and the baby when they returned to their room.

Like an airplane rolling down a well-lit runway came the bed with Katte returning from surgery. There were five nurses and assistants in tow as well as the new father. They were the surgical posse. Again, we were told to wait outside the room for a few more minutes until they got Katte set. At this point, we couldn't tell if the baby was in the bed with her because Katte was turned a bit on her left side, away from where we were standing. Even though our wait continued a little longer, we were filled with joy, happiness, and eagerness. We felt and saw the victory of answered prayer! Praise God.

By this hour, it has been nearly a full day since Katte first entered the hospital in anticipation of my first grandbaby. I know my child is tired. But now she is relieved that the worst is over, at least until the teenage years.

When we were finally allowed back in the room, I charged ahead and led the way. My main concern was for Katte and knowing if my daughter was doing well. Her back was facing the door, so I rushed around the bed to greet her face-to-face on the other side. Katte smiled so softly. As tired as she was, she smiled and as she looked over her shoulder, wanting to be sure all the

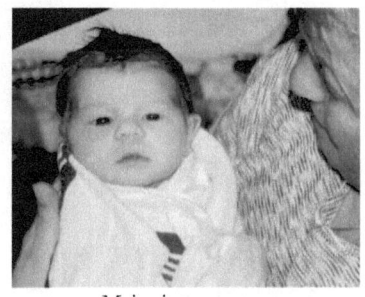

Maisy in my arms.

grandparents were present, spoke in a whisper, "Is everyone in here?" All who were still at the hospital were in the room. With that, Katte clutched the blanket in her right hand, and as she opened it, she announced, "Everyone... meet Maisy Rose."

Instantly, my attention and concern left my daughter and moved to that little swaddled bundle of joy. There she lay, cradled contently at her mother's side with her dark curly hair peeking out from under her cap. I lifted her out of the bed like a precious bouquet. As I brought her into my arms, I held her close to my chest, face, and neck. She was so soft and gentle. Her little face appeared more beautiful than the ultrasound images I saw during pregnancy. What a little slice of heaven appearing just for us.

After a few minutes, I said to the other grandma, "Here, Nancy, meet your new granddaughter." Then I passed Maisy off to her. At that time, I went back to Katte to show her my comfort and love. I was so proud of Katte and knew her poor body was close to exhaustion but filled with happiness and joy.

Maisy on the second day lay on her belly and held her head high. I knew she was destined for greatness.

Yes, Maisy is a promise, a miracle, and a blessing. I can only hope and imagine that all grandchildren are born with overwhelming joy for all the parents, including the awaiting grandparents, aunts, uncles, and friends. Maisy is my only grandchild to this day, and for me, she is enough.

My cup overflows.

Psalm 127:3-5 says, *"Children are a heritage from the LORD, offspring a reward from him. Like arrows in the hands of a warrior are children born in one's youth. Blessed is the man whose quiver is full of them."*

Maisy with her parents, Katte, and David. Aunt Kitte kissing her cheek. Aunt Jessica holding Maisy on her lap.

Legacies, Cookies, and Kool-Aid

Many children were raised with families going to church. Most of my people still attend church faithfully. These are some stories about notable pastors I have heard of or have experienced firsthand.

I've overheard narratives of the great orator, R. G. Lee, who preached for thirty-three years at Bellevue Baptist Church in Memphis, Tennessee, from 1927-1960. During that time, over 24,000 people joined the church and 7,600 were baptized. It was said that Pastor Lee often enjoyed a big bologna sandwich with a thick slice of onion. People commented, "You might not look like R.G., and you might not preach like R.G., but you can sure smell like him."

Charles Spurgeon, one of the greatest preachers of the 1800s, served in the Metropolitan Tabernacle of London. His tenure of thirty-eight years started when was only nineteen years old. At age twenty-two, he was already a popular preacher. His ability to preach the word of God with conviction made him famous as people flocked to the New Park Street Chapel. Soon the congregation outgrew the Chapel and moved to the Surrey Music Hall in London where 10,000 or more attended services each Sunday. Those were big numbers back in the 1800s.

His sermons were published and circulated for people to study. Eventually, Pastor Spurgeon printed over 3,600 sermons in 49 volumes of the *New Park Street Pulpit* publication. Unfortunately, the Reverend Charles Spurgeon died at age fifty-seven. Stories were told that he enjoyed a cup of hot cocoa and a cigar to settle down after his sermons. That sounds awful to me, but what do I know about cigars?

George W. Truett, served for forty-seven years as pastor of the First Baptist Church in Dallas back when automobiles were still a novelty. He insisted on riding in a horse-drawn carriage because he thought the horseless carriage would never catch on. For thirty-seven of those years, he went on cattle drives to preach the word to young men who were away from home for months at a time. Therefore, meat and beans were his staple. Essentially, Pastor Truett was a farm boy from Haysville, North Carolina, and the seventh child. In 1891, he went to work for Baylor University in Waco, Texas. Then two years later, he enrolled in Baylor, thus graduating in 1897. Upon graduation, he accepted the position at the First Baptist Church in Dallas. During his pastorate of forty-seven years, membership increased from 715 to 7,800. Over 19,000 new members joined the church. A total exceeding $6 million in tithes and offerings were raised during his tenure; thus, the church was expanded three times.

Pastor Bob Russell of the Louisville, Kentucky's Southwest Christian Church retired in 2006 after serving there for forty years. When he accepted the position, the church had a meager 120 members. At Pastor Russell's retirement, he served over 20,000 members. I drove near Southwest one Sunday after church, and there were multitudes of cars leaving the parking lots, ushered by many yellow-jacketed volunteers. Occasionally, while I lived in Scottsburg and attended the Scottsburg Christian Church, Pastor Russell was our guest preacher. Scottsburg was only thirty miles from Louisville. Yes, he was a dynamic presenter of God's word.

I remember the preacher of my childhood at Samaria Baptist Church in rural Paragon. His name was the Reverend Finkbinder. Samaria Church is not far from the Dow family farm. In fact, Philip and Patty, plus other family members, continue to attend Samaria Baptist Church. When I was young, I attended Samaria for Vacation Bible School (VBS). It was always held in the evenings. We lived in a farming community, and everyone worked during the day. The biggest draw for me as a child was the cookies and Kool-Aid. In essence, I came to know Jesus because of *cookies and Kool-*

Aid. I have never doubted my roots and have grown in my Christian faith from there. Thank God for the small community churches who feed the children both physically and spiritually. May it always be they learn the stories of the Bible while having fun snacks.

Samaria Baptist where I was raised and gave my life to Jesus.

Now, my most recent pastor has been Chris Philbeck of Mount Pleasant Christian Church in Greenwood. Pastor Chris has pastored me since 2008, and I have grown exponentially in my faith under his teaching. He retired as of June 30, 2024. That Sunday afternoon the church hosted a huge picnic celebrating our pastor and his family. It was a catered event in a huge white tent full of tables. Plus, there were tables and chairs inside the gymnasium. Over 2,000 parishioners were present for the sendoff. I was one of them. In his forty-five years as a pastor, Chris served three congregations, including twenty-three years at Mount Pleasant. Yes, we will miss Pastor Chris deeply. His impact touched thousands over his tenure.

What a legacy these spiritual leaders have made and the impact they left for the generations to come. Oh, that each of us could make such an impact. Who knows, maybe we do.

Never second guess the impression your faith makes in the world around you. You are more of an influence than you realize. May the blessing of faith follow you and spill out on others all the days of your life.

Jesus always wants us to come to him. Do you realize that God only has sons and daughters. No granddaughters or grandsons or any other relationship, only sons and daughters. Furthermore, He wants us to come to faith in Him at any age. Just like the scripture below:

Matthew 19:14 Jesus said, *"Let the little children come to me, and do not hinder them, for the kingdom of heaven belongs to such as these."*

Holidays
and
Days to Remember

Resolutions and Goals

"Out with the old and in the with the new!" A lot of us make "New Year's resolutions." My experience with these, it's not long until they are all broken. Resolutions can be like vapor. We have good intentions when we pen them; however, without step-by-step plans for our goals, we often fail. Unfortunately, failing enough times, we stop trying. By not trying, we stop attempting to resolve, to change, or improve anything. Is that the answer to making our lives better? No, God forbid it ever be! We must persevere at all ages to improve ourselves.

Dearly beloved, we need God's grace to forgive ourselves and others when failing to reach our resolutions. I am still looking at a few to master. Before writing goals, one must decide why we want or need change. What is it about our current lifestyles that need resolving? When we know the *why*, the bite size steps become crystal clear. Let me say this, people survive every year without making New Year's resolutions. If that is you, well, thank you for reading this article.

Age brings failing health. All those years of making a resolution of losing weight, trying to get fit, and have better health was a good goal but never fully attained. Now, it is of paramount importance to find a resolve and settle it for you mental well-being, if you can.

One year, in the third week of November, I was awakened to the rapid beating of my heart. It was palpitating for reasons unknown. Taking my pulse in my neck was to no avail as I couldn't count the irregular rhythm. It was beating like Morse code. My phone nor my iPad were near me while I lay in bed, so I couldn't call anyone. Remembering how settling deep breathing can be, I tried that. Nope, the race was still on. Having high blood pressure which can make me light-headed upon rising, I chose to remain lying in bed. I said a prayer to God to please fix it or take me home, then I turned on the television for a distraction. Hours later, I woke up to a regular heart rate, and a huge wake-up call. I must get this midnight excitement checked out by the medical profession.

After three different doctor visits, labs, echograms, stress tests, a thirty-day heart monitor, and sleep study tests, it was determined that I have sleep apnea. It seems I am in good company. So now, I get to have this contraption on my face every night. "They" say I will get used to it and love it as time goes by. It's been a week, and I am still looking for the love. Now five years later and forty-seven pounds lighter, I no longer need to have the CPAP machine because the added weight is gone. The doctor said to keep the machine in case I gain the weight back, and I need it again. I'm resolved to never gain it back. In fact, I am trying to lose a few more pounds for good measure.

Another time, for three years, I received cortisone shots in my knee. After the shot, my knee was fine if I didn't walk downstairs, or play pickleball, or golf, or walk too much. Fortunately, or unfortunately, I live an active lifestyle. To continue with the activities I desire, I must get a new knee, as arthritis is not my friend. That is a gift that keeps on giving from my mother and grandmother. Their bodies were riddled with arthritis. My buddies at pickleball are so kind. They tell me many people bounce back quickly from joint replacement. (I think they had their fingers crossed behind their backs, a sign of fibbing.) They mentioned that the older we become, the harder it is to bounce. I attest to that. I don't rebound well; my experience is more like a thud. So, a new knee happened in May 2019. Oh Joy! It has been a true joy, and now my limitations are only about 5 percent. In other words, I can use my knee for 95 percent of what I could do as a kid. (If I wanted to.)

Now comes the research. I googled "How to lose belly fat." Besides the obvious, I want a quick fix. So here it is. My resolution, to lose pounds and strengthen my core. They listed six *simple steps*. Nothing is easy, or I would already be doing it. First, get rid of sugar, especially in drinks. It causes belly fat and harm to the liver. Second, eat more protein. Protein satisfies hunger and reduces cravings. Be sure to include fish, seafood, beans, nuts, meat, and dairy. Third, cut carbs to no more than fifty grams daily. What does that look like? I will need to get a carb counter book. Supposedly, it gets rid of belly and organ fat. Fourth, increase fiber, especially fruits and vegetables, the crunchy ones. Fiber absorbs fat and helps flush it away. Fifth, exercise extends your life and avoid disease. Walking is king, so walk. Walking is good unless you have arthritis in your feet. Then I chose to walk in the water. While on vacations, I walk more than normal and most generally lose weight. We will always need to walk our whole lifetime, so practice walking. Every hour, get out of that chair and go for a walk. Okay, maybe every two hours. Sixth and last, track your intake and exercise. There once was a free app on my phone called "My Fitness Pal." It tracked everything, even nutrients and fitness. Maybe I will try it.

Consequently, I've decided that will be my plan, and I am sticking to it. Even a month at a time, as my friend Rick said, "A monthly goal revisited is a good goal." Please make this and every new year your best yet! As we press on to the future, it may as well be positive and healthy. Like it says in Hebrews 12:1–2 *"...And let us run with perseverance the race marked out for us, fixing our eyes on Jesus, the pioneer and perfecter of faith..."*

Green on Saint Patrick's Day

Have you ever wondered, "Who is St. Patrick and why do we celebrate his day?" I couldn't remember if he was the guy who led all the rats to drown in the river. Or maybe he had something to do with potatoes. Inquiring minds need to know, so I did a little research.

I graduated from Martinsville High School, but that was a few years ago. Surely, we were taught something about Ireland, if so, I missed it. All I remembered is if I didn't wear green on St. Patrick's Day, I got pinched. I was sure to wear green because getting pinched didn't seem like fun to me.

St. Patrick was born AD 387 to a wealthy family in Kilpatrick, Scotland. His birth name was Maewyn Succat. (Yikes, I'd change my name to Patrick too.) History records show at age sixteen he was captured by Irish raiders and spent several years in Ireland as a slave. Eventually, he escaped by ship and went back to Scotland. As I kept researching, it was the Pied Piper who played his pipe luring rats out of the city to drown in the river. Though it was a legend, still the Pied Piper is depicted on many churches' stained-glass windows in the United Kingdom. But that was a different time and place. Pied means multicolored not green, for your information.

Meanwhile, after St. Patrick's conversion to Christianity, he returned to Ireland to witness for Jesus Christ. Though he was never canonized a saint, he was a bishop. As a missionary for more than thirty years, he converted over 135,000 people to Christianity. While establishing 300 churches, he consecrated 350 bishops. St. Patrick was filled with the spirit of God throughout his life. As you know, St. Patrick's Day takes on many faces in today's world. There is the leprechaun and his lucky charms. The three leaf shamrocks which are supposed to bring good luck. I always thought that the four-leaf clover was lucky. Of course, the specialty foods and green alcoholic drinks are plentiful when celebrating St. Patrick's Day. Most large cities have a parade with the participants and onlookers dressed in green attire. Some cities even color their rivers and canals green for the day.

St. Patrick took many Celtic symbols and made them Christian. For example, he took the shamrock and let it be a symbol for the Trinity— Father, Son, and the Holy Spirit. He died on March 17, AD 461 at the age of seventy-four. Because of his service to the multitudes during their hardships, Ireland named March 17th a national holiday in his honor. Currently, no one works on March 17 in Ireland. What started as a religious holiday has now become a secular holiday exhibiting plenty of Irish culture in green throughout the world.

During the seventeenth, eighteenth, and nineteenth centuries, hundreds of thousands of Irish people immigrated to New York City looking for a new and better way of life. Unfortunately, they became indentured servants to the ones who booked their passage to sail. Eventually, they got their debt paid and became free. Consequently, New York City was a hot bed of Irish and had its first annual St. Patrick's Day parade in 1762. Not long after, many Irish were recruited to help the North win the Civil War. Although they were not eager to go to war, they were against slavery. They knew all too well the job of being an indentured servant because many had firsthand experience.

Most of us living in the United States today have never experienced real hunger. Just the opposite, we have trouble overeating. However, the Irish had been hungry for centuries. There were many famines because England took their potatoes and other produce as well as life stock for exports to other countries. For example, the Irish famine in 1740 killed 400,000 people. They endured a starvation holocaust which was repeated many times. Even with the overwhelming influence of St. Patrick back in the three-digit years, the country was filled with poverty. During the early Middle Ages, Irish churches were exceedingly poor, even their Catholic leadership had no political clout. Many leaders converted to Presbyterian and to the Anglican Church of Ireland to get away from the Church of England. Finally in 1921, Ireland secured their independence from England.

So why do we wear green on St. Paddy's Day? Ireland is called the "Emerald Isle" for lo, 'tis so green. Green symbolizes Irish culture and the onset of spring. That's why you notice Laddies and Lassies wearing Kelly green on March 17. All of this sounds like a good enough reason to me, but I still don't understand the pinching penalty.

Above all, remember this, St. Patrick was a fine Scotsman who ministered to Ireland all his adult life.

Memorial Day and the Indy 500

Do you recall when Memorial Day was called "Decoration Day?" It's a federal holiday to remember and honor those who died while serving in the armed forces. Essentially, it began after the Civil War. From 1868 to 1970, Memorial Day was May 30 regardless of what day of the week it fell on. Unofficially, this marked the first day of summer. However, in 1971, the last Monday of May was designated as Memorial Day.

Some pay respect to fallen heroes and other loved ones by decorating their graves. Or at least visit the cemetery. If nothing else, pull the overgrowth surrounding away from their grave markers. I hope someone honors me someday, but not too soon.

Indianapolis, Indiana, has a little race every year that used to fall on Monday, Memorial Day. The problem was, if it rained, many fans may not return the next day for the restart. (Tuesday is always a workday.) These high-powered race cars hydroplane so easily when the track is wet. For safety sake, they stop the race when it rains. Since 1974, the race has been held on Sunday, the day prior to Memorial Day, returning on Monday if needed.

The 500-mile race started in 1911 and has become the "Greatest spectacle in racing!" Two weeks prior to the race weekend, the drivers practice and fine-tune their cars. To qualify for the race, the driver must be one of the thirty-three fastest for those timed trial laps. The timed trials is a method of placing the cars into the thirty-three positions. The field has eleven rows of three cars. The inside of the first row sits the fastest car on the first day of qualification runs. That position of honor is called *pole position*. The driver that sits on the pole gets plenty of attention and a bonus paycheck for the award.

The racers drive their cars on a four-lap timed trial equaling ten miles to garner an average lap speed. Timed trials take place the two weekends before the race. Many people go to the timed trials every year but never the race. That has always been a mystery to me, but it is a true statement.

The race itself consists of driving counterclockwise around a rectangular track with four steep-banked rounded turns. The track is two and a half miles in length. Going around for 200 laps equals 500 miles. See how good I can be at math? Many of you already know these facts and could recite them better than I am doing, but please bear in mind that not everyone knows the details.

Let's talk about the racing cars. The Indianapolis Motor Speedway has been referred to as the *proving grounds*. Many improvements in the auto industry have developed through racing. Often, various tire and other auto industry companies perform test drives on the track. Numerous positive changes have come about as a result. The rigors of driving puts oil, air filters, and the like through their paces during a race. Often, there are cars running around the track during the off season for that very purpose, testing various parts on the car.

The race is contested by "Indy cars," a single-seat, open-cockpit, open-wheel, purposed race car. As of 2018, all entrants utilize a 2.2L V-6, twin-turbo charged engines. They produce a range of 550-700 horsepower. Primarily Chevrolet and Honda engines are used currently. The 2012 Chassis made by Dallara of Italy, who is the sole supplier of chassis.

Here's a little trivia. Dan Weldon was Dallara's test driver. After Dan was killed racing at the Las Vegas Motor Speedway in October 2011, they named the car after him. All tires used are made by Firestone. Seems to me there's a monopoly going on there at the track. Of course, they have proven themselves. Something better will come along.

Let's get personal. My first race was 1966 when Graham Hill won. It was quite a thrill for this young farm girl. The biggest thing I had ever done prior to that was go to the state fair. I have been to eighteen races and will only go now if I am chaperoning someone to their first experience or they are visiting from out of town.

There is nothing like the experience of the opening ceremonies of this event. My body chills all over, the hairs stand up on my arms, and my eyes well up with tears from the excitement. A lump in my throat develops as the events unfold. Go to it just once, you will feel the rumble in your soul as the cars go by on their parade laps following the pace car.

Then the green flag drops and here they come, all thirty-three cars screaming their high-pitched engines. The engines reverberate through my soul and body. Sitting on the outside of the track is the best and especially in a turn. The thrill is quite possibly one of the finest in all sports. Like I said, I'd rather not go and fight the crowd. However, if I am taking a friend to the race who has never been, it is a thrill just watching their first experience.

Georgiann and Laura at the race in 2023, my guests

My first husband has been to every race since 1953 when his dad first started taking him. My daughters started going with their dad in 1978 and have rarely missed a race. Now, my granddaughter Maisy, started going in 2015 as the fourth generation to follow the tradition. It's a happy time for them to share the memory and the moments.

Enjoy your Memorial Day with family and friends however you choose to celebrate. There is nothing quite like having traditional activities to remember as we grow old.

Paying it Forward on Father's Day

Have you heard the story that happened on Father's Day in June 2017? It took place in the small town of Scottsburg, Indiana. When I heard this story, my interest piqued. As one does at times like these, I googled the story, and there it was. Without a doubt, you have heard of these kinds of things happening elsewhere I'm sure.

My career took me to that thriving and quaint southern Indiana town for a duration of almost ten years beginning in 1996. For your information, Scottsburg is twenty-nine miles north of Louisville, Kentucky, on Interstate 65. The population is around 6,700. They are known for being friendly yet very laid back. One might say it is a sleepy small town with lots of character. I know I genuinely enjoyed my time while I lived and worked in and around Scottsburg. I made numerous friends, and we remain friends to this day.

Apparently, one rainy night at 8:30, a lady was placing her order at the McDonald's drive-through. She noticed a man behind her with his van full of children. Since it was Father's Day, after she paid for her order, she said, "I'd like to purchase the order for the man in the van behind me as well." She told the gal at the window, "Please tell him happy Father's Day for me and to enjoy his children."

Her order was number forty-five. That gesture continued until closing time at midnight. In total, 167 consecutive customers paid it forward on that rainy Father's Day night in Scottsburg. They paid for the car behind them. The truth was the workers were ecstatic by the kindness spreading from stranger to stranger the rest of the night. They watched to see if the streak would be broken.

After over 100 patrons had gone through, a customer wasn't going to pay for the car behind, so the workers pooled their money and paid the check to see if the trend would continue. It did—until closing time. In fact, the last person was sad they could not pay it forward. However, there was always tomorrow to start a new chain of paying it forward.

Can you imagine the delight of all the customers on that Father's Day receiving their free meal that night? Plus, the joyful generosity by paying for someone else's bill. Have you ever paid it forward like that, or performed a random act of kindness? I have but usually only to people I know. I remember in 2011 while on a girl's trip in Destin, Florida, two carloads of us went through Starbucks. My car was in front, and I paid for the girls in the second car. From that day forward, those crazy girls always wanted me to be the lead car. Those old heifers!

My sister Carol was driving on Highway 31 in Greenwood one time when a car darted in front of her. She had to slam on her brakes to keep from hitting them. Then the car pulled off the road into the McDonald's drive-through. It just so happened that Carol was going to the drive-through at McDonald's as well. When she got up to the window to pay, the guy who cut her off had paid for her order and left a message. "Please tell her I'm sorry I cut you off on 31, forgive me and enjoy your order." That made her day to hear the message and get her free meal.

The list is endless of the various *random acts of kindness* we can pay to others. Practice these acts long enough, and they become habit—a way of life. Most random acts have small dollar values. For example, letting someone go ahead of you in line. That is a big one, we always want to be first. Other things like holding a door, or smiling, or helping a neighbor, checking on someone after an illness, being the first one to speak, and acts like that. Those are all random acts which don't cost a thing but a little kindness.

The season for giving is ongoing, and thus, we might want to take the high road and think more of others than ourselves when out shopping or otherwise running errands.

It feels good, and rarely ever hurts us. In fact, we are overly blessed when we do.

In the 2000 movie *Pay It Forward*, the challenge was when you did something for someone, instead of paying you back, it was suggested they do something for three other people instead. That was the first time I had heard of the phrase, *pay it forward*.

The idea of random acts of kindness has been around for a long time. Just like feeding the hungry, they are hungry *every* day. However, many people do something kind for the foodbanks only during the holidays.

This scripture applies to this situation and many like it. Luke 6:38 says, "Give, and it will be given to you. A good measure, pressed down, shaken together, and running over will be poured into your lap. For with the measure you use, it will be measured back to you."

I hope you always pay it forward in many ways. You might choose random or purposeful acts of kindness. It is never too late to begin or begin again. Those workers and patrons at McDonald's didn't question taking part in doing a little *something* to make someone's day. We can do the same if we make a little effort.

In the meantime, spread a little sunshine every day and don't forget to smile at all the people you meet and greet. You just might make their day. My challenge to you is to do what you can, all the time. Make it a way of life. By doing so, your own cup will be overflowing with blessings unexpected. The scripture in Luke supports this attitude:

"Give, and it will be given to you. A good measure, pressed down, shaken together, and running over, will be poured into your lap. For with the measure you use, it will be measured to you"(Luke 6:38).

9/11 and Red-Letter Days

Ask anyone where they were when the planes struck the World Trade Center in New York City on September 11, 2001. They will remember. The people of America hadn't had anything so disruptive in their world since JFK (President John F. Kennedy) was shot. Before that, it was the bombing of Pearl Harbor. I call these events "Red-Letter Days."

The twin towers struck on 9/11/2001

With the anniversary of that horrible event of 9/11, we vividly recall how it affected each of us. Most people reading this article are aware of the events surrounding that fateful day. I was in Florida preparing to fly home from a vacation. While watching television that morning, once the first plane had reportedly struck the tower, my eyes were glued to the television for the rest of the day. All flights were grounded.

After three days with no flights, my companion and I rented a car to drive home to Indiana. We needed to get back for work. Unfortunately, the only thing playing on the car radio was info regarding the terrorists attacks.

Typically, in 2001, over 1.6 million people flew on 36-40,000 flights per day. A screeching halt to all flights was mandated when the terrorists slammed the hijacked jet into the second tower of the World Trade Center. Soon, all major airports in the USA were locked down until further notice. The northeastern corridor of Amtrak train service was canceled. Greyhound bus lines suspended their operations around the country as well.

All international flights enroute to the states were rerouted to the nearest airports. You may remember the stories about 6,700 passengers grounded in Gander, Newfoundland. The population of Gander was less than ten thousand people in 2001. Several passengers were treated as special houseguests by their residents. Every church, school, and gymnasium was filled with makeshift shelters. Gander became known as casserole city for the thirty-eight flights that landed there. Incredible yet graceful gestures were shown by the whole people of Gander. Additionally, other smaller Canadian airports took in many grounded flights.

Some of the incoming European and Asian flights who weren't halfway to the US were directed to return to their departure airports. On the West Coast, Vancouver's airports were flooded with grounded flights. It was a scary mess causing our spirits to be frozen in time.

Driving back from Florida, my personal car was parked in the garage adjacent to the airport terminal in Louisville, Kentucky. Upon arrival, we noticed the garage was empty. Authorities were skeptical of the parked cars being so close to their terminal. They towed all cars to an out lot, situated end to end. Not only was it difficult to find my car, but it also took two hours to retrieve it from the mess of parked cars crammed so close together.

Another red-letter day was assassination of President John F. Kennedy. It caused a similar paralysis throughout the country as did 9/11. The patriotism shown   for these two occurrences makes one proud to be an American. Our country was high on life with the leadership shown by JFK. Then he was gone. I was only a young teen at the time.

I wasn't around for the Pearl Harbor, or the Normandy Beach attacks, but I have visited both sites. Reading all the history of both makes me believe that war is not a good method to solve conflict. But it is here to stay. In fact, we read in Matthew 24:6 where Jesus says, "And you will hear of wars and rumors of war. See that you are not alarmed, for this must take place, but the end is not yet." That is not very reassuring, but it is true.

The fact is, we have always had conflict since the beginning of time. Maybe a better endeavor would be to find constructive and positive ways to deal with discord. Try a little kindness would be a start. "A soft answer turns away wrath, but a harsh word stirs up anger" (Proverbs 15:1).

Other personal red-letter days would be any monumental moments which are life-changing in one way or another. They are usually things of great accomplishment or achievement. For example, I trained for and ran the "500" mini-marathon road race in 1984. That memory still feels good.

Before that, the birth of my daughters making me a mother was quite a feat. For some, that might not seem like a red-letter day, but to me, it was a stamp of approval by God. I am now in charge of another life. That job seemed to run out just when I was getting good at it, but they still make me proud.

Above all, *never forget* these acts of terror on our country. Many people have paid and gave it all, their life, for our freedom. Always remember to honor even the least sacrifice. I believe honoring those who served is deserving.

Remember now and forever all the promises of God. If God is for us, who can be against us. With that in mind, our fears should never be in the forefront of our minds. Go in peace and make the world a better place as far as it depends on you.

The end.

Additional photos

The girls and me on our Alaska trip in 2013

Kitte, Jessica and Katte in Alaska

Maisy and me at the Mendenhall Glacier in Juneau, Alaska

Philip, George, Carol, Phyllis, and Lois

Philip and George at the Morgan County fairgrounds
for the traveling Vietnam wall

Credits

All photos are from personal albums:
Katte and David Hanner
Kitte and Mike Allen
Jessica Bex
Maisy Rose Hanner
George Dow
Carol Teague
Philip Dow
Georgiann Harpe
Eva Haubry
Marilyn Duran
Patty Russell
Judy Speer
Laura Kovicich
Daphna Tobey
Donna Rector
Ron Sample
Jeffrey Walgreen
Evan Walgreen
Lisa Miller

About the Author

Phyllis Dow Bex has been a freelance writer since 2018 and authored her first book in February 2024 titled *Life on Turkeyneck Hill: A Memoir*. Primarily, her early work before her first book was that of providing weekly newspaper columns in her hometown where she grew up. She also provides quarterly columns in a boomer-aged magazine. In July 2024, Phyllis authored a second book, *More Tales from Turkeyneck Hill*. Now her third book is here.

Phyllis has always had a desire for learning new things and thus enabled her to express a wide range of interesting topics to use as a basis for her stories. Plus, her thirty-five years of selling insurance in a worksite marketing arena as well as the private in-home sales allowed her to meet colorful personalities and hear a variety of tales. These experiences have been the springboard for many of her columns and stories. Besides all of this, Phyllis has the knack to find humor in most situations and can put it in her word pictures for all to enjoy.

She is the mother of three adult daughters, two sons-in-law, and one favorite grandchild, Maisy Rose. Any time she spends with any of them is precious.

Now in her quiet and full retirement years, Phyllis writes. She writes notes on her phone and scraps of paper as a reference for later columns and books. In the meantime, she has time to travel, play golf, pickleball, table games, and generally enjoys conversations and new friendships along the way. Please enjoy.

**Additional books coming soon,
authored by
Phyllis Dow Bex:**

*Miliary Legacies: Family and Friends Who Have
Served*

Traveling Journals from a Country Girls Perspective

A Hoosier in the Holy Land

www.ingramcontent.com/pod-product-compliance
Lightning Source LLC
Chambersburg PA
CBHW021137130626
46554CB00005B/1553